The Power of NONVIOLENCE

THE POWER OF
Nonviolence

RICHARD B. GREGG

SCHOCKEN BOOKS · NEW YORK

First SCHOCKEN edition 1966

Fourth Printing, 1971

Published by arrangement with the Fellowship
of Reconciliation, Nyack, N. Y.

Library of Congress Catalog Card No. 66-24905

Manufactured in the United States of America

TO

MOHANDAS KARAMCHAND GANDHI

CONTENTS

PREFACE

THERE WILL always be conflicts, great and small, in human affairs. The H-bomb has made it obvious that total war can no longer settle conflicts. And clearly no conflict can be ended in its inner reality by the alleged deterrence from the possession of nuclear weapons. In such a stalemate the possibility of using nonviolent resistance might be worth examining.

At first mention, the term "nonviolent resistance" seems self-contradictory. How can any resistance be effective in this modern world unless it has in it and backing it up, great strength, power and, if need be, weapons? At least a threat of violence seems an essential of resistance. Nevertheless, there have been instances in history where great courage, deep conviction and a fine cause have prevailed, without violence, against armed might. Gandhi's struggle for the freedom of India was one instance. In this book we shall examine the nature of the force used in such instances, and see whether it can be applied to other conflict situations.

The unity of the human species is not only a biological and physiological fact; it is, when wisely and fully asserted and acted upon, a great power. Human unity is actual in man's universal capacity to think, feel, will, understand and act, and to apprehend spiritual truths. Human unity is a power that can overcome all differences of race, nationality, ideology or culture. Military leaders have aroused partial unity by means of fear, pride, anger, hate and lies. But unity can also be aroused, more fruitfully and enduringly, by love and the desire for justice. This book is a partial examination of how and why human unity can help solve human conflicts.

Is nonviolent resistance intellectually and morally respectable or not? If it is at all practical anywhere, to what extent, and why? Is it applicable in the West, or not?

It is difficult for one trained in modern Western modes of thought and action to understand this idea or to believe that its practice can be cogent. Even Gandhi's explanations of it fail to carry weight with most of us. His explanations come out of a background of thought, feeling and attitude to life very different from ours. The assumptions of Indians are different, and so are their social experiences, the elements of thought which are implicit but never definitely stated, their historical allusions, their analogies and figures of speech. Therefore I have felt it desirable to restate and explain this method in modern Western concepts and terminology.

I have not limited the explanation merely to Gandhi's own concepts or to India, but have tried to explain and evaluate the principle in its application in any country, at any time, under any circumstances and for any cause. I have attempted to show why persuasion of this sort is more powerful and more permanently advantageous than physical coercion.

If we want a better world, we must be prepared to do some careful thinking. It is time we stopped being sketchy on a matter that touches us all so closely. For in reality this matter of handling conflict constructively is of immediate concern to everyone who has ever been angry or afraid, resentful, revengeful or bitter; who has ever taken part in a fight, mob violence or war; or who has been the object of anger, hatred, exploitation or oppression. It touches all those who are troubled lest the vast economic, political and social questions that are pressing upon all nations will issue in still more appalling violence and increased insecurity for everyone, or even destruction of the human race. It is also important to those who hope that somehow the ideals of mankind can be made practical and harmonized with its conduct.

My qualifications for writing this book are experiences of conflict involved in my three years' practice of law and seven years in industrial relations work, followed by a stay in India of nearly four years beginning early in 1925, of which about seven months altogether were spent at Gandhi's own *ashram* at Sabarmati, another six-week visit to India in March and April, 1930, another visit there of about the same length in the winter of 1949-50, and eighteen months of teaching, writing and travel in India in 1956-1958, many discussions with Gandhi and a careful study of most of what he wrote, so far as I could find it; also a study of much of the other literature of the entire subject of conflict and peace.

To all the clear, profound and sensitive minds with which I have come in contact, in India and in other countries, in the past and the present, I owe a great obligation. To Gandhi especially I am grateful. For criticism and help I desire to thank especially my wife, W. Norman Brown, Caroline F. Tupper, Blanche Watson, John Nevin Sayre, the late Rufus M. Jones, my sister, Marjorie T. Gregg, Alfred Hassler, William Robert Miller and the late C. F. Andrews. I want also to thank all the authors and publishers who have kindly permitted me to quote from their books and articles.

The first edition of this book was published in 1934. It was revised in 1944 and now events since then call for another revision.

RICHARD B. GREGG

Chester, N. Y.
November 1958

The Power of NONVIOLENCE

1

MODERN EXAMPLES OF NONVIOLENT RESISTANCE

THERE HAVE BEEN many instances of the successful use of non-violent resistance in different countries and at different times. Because the taste of historians inclines more toward politics and wars, these other events have received but slight attention at their hands, and the records of many of them have been lost. In some instances the nonviolent resistance was by individuals, in other instances it took a mass or corporate form. The latter form is rarer and perhaps more significant. For this reason and because this book is not primarily a history, I will attempt to tell of only a few outstanding successful modern examples of the latter sort.

HUNGARY

THE FIRST TO BE considered occurred in Hungary during the mid-nineteenth century.[1] The emperor Franz Josef was trying to subordinate Hungary to the Austrian power, contrary to the terms of the old treaty of union of those two countries. The Hungarian moderates felt helpless, as they were too weak to fight. But Ferenc Deak, a Catholic landowner of Hungary, protested to them: "Your laws are violated, yet your mouths remain closed! Woe to the nation that raises no protest when its rights are outraged! It contributes to its own slavery by its silence. The nation that submits to injustice and oppression without protest is doomed."

Deak proceeded to organize a scheme for independent Hungarian education, agriculture and industry, a refusal to recognize the Austrian government in any way, and a boycott against Austrian goods. He admonished the people not to be betrayed into acts of violence, nor to abandon the ground of legality. "This is the safe ground," he said, "on which, unarmed ourselves, we can hold our own against armed force. If suffering must be necessary, suffer with dignity."

The advice was obeyed throughout Hungary. When the Austrian tax collector came, the people did not beat him or even hoot him— they merely declined to pay. The Austrian police then seized their goods, but no Hungarian auctioneer would sell them. When an Austrian auctioneer was brought, he found that he would have to bring bidders from Austria. The government soon discovered that it was costing more to distrain the property than the tax was worth.

The Austrians attempted to billet their soldiers upon the Hungarians. The Hungarians did not actively resist the order, but the Austrian soldiers, after trying to live in houses where everyone despised them, protested strongly against it. The Austrian government declared the boycott of Austrian goods illegal, but the Hungarians defied the decree. The jails were filled to overflowing. No representatives from Hungary would sit in the Imperial Parliament.

The Austrians then tried conciliation. The prisoners were released and partial self-government given. But Hungary insisted upon its full claims. In reply, Emperor Franz Josef decreed compulsory military service. The Hungarians answered that they would refuse to obey it. Finally, on February 18, 1867, the Emperor capitulated and gave Hungary her constitution.

The campaign seems to have been defective because of some violence of inner attitude on the part of the Hungarians. But even so, it provided a remarkable example of the power of nonviolent resistance, even though the principle was imperfectly realized and applied.

SOUTH AFRICA

THE NEXT EXAMPLE occurred in South Africa. It lasted eight years, beginning in 1906. For many years previously, Indians had been coming to Natal as manual workers in the mines and elsewhere, originally at the invitation of the Europeans who wished to develop the country. Many thousands of the Indians came as indentured laborers, whose term of service was five years. They were industrious, entered into farming and trade, and thereby began to compete with the Europeans. By 1906 some 12,500 of them had crossed the border and settled in the Transvaal. They were subject to many unfair laws.

In 1906, the Transvaal government introduced a bill in the legislature which would require every Indian to be registered by fingerprint, like criminals, and to produce his certificate of registration upon demand of any police officer at any time. Failure to register meant deportation, and refusal to produce the certificate would be punished by fine.

The Indians had always been subject to severe restrictions, but this proposal meant their complete subjection and probably their destruction as a community. Under the leadership of an Indian lawyer, M. K. Gandhi, they held meetings of protest and asked for hearings on the bill. But the government said no and passed the bill. Thereupon the leading Indians, at a huge mass meeting, took an oath that they would all refuse to register and would go to jail rather than obey a law that they regarded as an attack upon the very foundations of their religion, their national honor and their self-respect.

They stuck to their resolve, and Gandhi and many others went to jail. The Prime Minister, General Jan Christian Smuts, then undertook to have the law repealed if the Indians would register voluntarily. The Indians agreed and did their part, but General Smuts did not carry out his side of the agreement. Moreover, the government introduced a further bill which applied the old registration law to all Asians who had not registered voluntarily. The Indians then resolved to renew the struggle.

Not long after, in 1913, a European judge in the Transvaal Supreme Court made a court decision that invalidated all Hindu and Mohammedan marriages, thus rendering all Indian children illegitimate and incapable of inheriting property. This roused the Indian women. A group of them, at Gandhi's suggestion, crossed from the Transvaal into Natal, and picketed the Natal mines, which were worked by Indian laborers. Since Indians were forbidden by law to cross the boundary without permission, the women were imprisoned. The men, numbering about five thousand, all came out on strike as a protest. Under Gandhi's leadership they proposed to march on foot across the border into the Transvaal, by way of a nonviolent protest.

Gandhi notified the Government of this proposed action and asked for a revocation of the law, several days before the march, and again just before it started, but to no effect.

They marched, some four thousand strong, about twenty-five miles a day, living on the charity of Indian merchants. During the march

Gandhi was arrested three times, released on bail twice, and finally put in jail. The border was crossed and the army continued, leaderless, but still nonviolent. Finally they were all arrested and taken back by train to Natal. They were impounded at the mines and beaten and ill-treated. Still they remained firm and nonviolent.

This brutal affair aroused a tremendous storm of public opinion both in South Africa and India. Lord Hardinge, the Viceroy of India, in a public speech at Madras, praised and defended the conduct of the nonviolent resisters and protested against the acts of the Union of South Africa. Two Englishmen, C. F. Andrews and W. W. Pearson, went to South Africa from India at the request of the Indian public. Later, the Viceroy sent Sir Benjamin Robertson to represent the Government of India. But the negotiations with the protesting Indians remained entirely in Gandhi's hands.

General Smuts, seeing that he had to retreat, appointed a committee of investigation to save the face of the government, and at the same time released Gandhi and two other leaders of the Indians. The Indians requested representation on the committee as surety of good faith. When Smuts refused, Gandhi prepared to renew the struggle.

Just then a strike broke out among the European railwaymen in South Africa. Gandhi saw that the government was in a very difficult situation, but instead of taking advantage of the incident, he chivalrously suspended the Indian struggle until the railway strike was over, an act that won much admiration for the Indians.

After the strike ended, Smuts found it necessary to yield, and the Indians won all the major parts of their demands: namely, the abolition of the registration, the abolition of the three-pound head-tax, the validation of their marriages, the right of entry of educated Indians, and an assurance of just administration of existing laws. Thus the whole struggle was won by nonviolent resistance.[2]

INDIA: CHAMPARAN

IN CHAMPARAN, northern India, in 1917, the peasants had been compelled by law to plant 15 percent of all their land in indigo and also were subject to other oppressive exactions by the planters. Gandhi, who had returned to live in India in 1914, was invited to investigate the conditions of the workers on the indigo plantations and the treatment given them by their employers. He began his inquiry without publicity, but the planters much resented his activities there and persuaded the district magistrate that the presence of Gandhi was dangerous to the peace of the district. The magistrate served an order upon Gandhi to leave the district by the next available train. Gandhi replied that he had come there from a sense of duty, that nothing was being done except carefully and quietly to ascertain facts, and that he would stay and, if necessary, submit to the penalty for disobedience.

He and his companions then proceeded quietly to take down in writing the statements of the peasants who came flocking to tell of their grievances. The witnesses were questioned to elicit the exact truth. The government sent police officers who were present at these proceedings and took notes of what happened. Gandhi and his assistants arranged that if he should be jailed or deported, two of them would go on taking the peasants' testimony; and if those two were arrested, then two more should take up the work, and so on.

Gandhi was summoned to court and tried. He simply pleaded guilty, and stated that he was faced with a conflict of duty—whether to obey the law or his conscience and the humane purposes for which he had come—and that under the circumstances he could only throw the responsibility of removing him upon the administration. The magistrate postponed judgment, and before it was rendered the lieutenant-governor gave orders that Gandhi should be permitted to proceed with the investigation. Then the governor of the province interested himself in the case and, after conferring with Gandhi, appointed a government commission of inquiry with Gandhi as a member. The commission reported unanimously that the law was unfair and the exactions of the big planters unjust. The law was repealed and justice given to the peasants. All this was wholly nonviolent.[3] This was a struggle for economic justice, with no political implications.

INDIA: VYKOM

ANOTHER NONVIOLENT struggle, this time for social rights, took place in a village called Vykom, in the State of Travancore in southern India. It was also directed by Gandhi, through some of his followers. A highway ran through the low-lying country around Vykom and through the village and close by the Brahman quarter and a temple. For centuries the Brahmans had refused to permit any low-caste "untouchable" people to use this road. The followers of Gandhi decided that this custom must be ended and the road thrown open to all human beings alike. Gandhi was ill, many hundred miles away, but the young leaders came north to consult with him, and as the campaign proceeded he instructed them by letters and telegrams from his sickbed. Later he visited Vykom personally.

The leaders started the struggle by taking several of the "untouchable" friends with them along this road and into the Brahman quarter. They were immediately beaten by the Brahmans, and one was seriously hurt. But the young reformers offered no violence in return. Then the police arrested several of these young men for encouraging trespass. They were condemned to prison for different periods of time, up to one year. At once, volunteers came pouring in from all parts of the country to take the place of those who were arrested. The State then forbade any further arrests but ordered the police to prevent any more of the reformers from entering the road. The police formed a cordon across the road. Thereupon, by instructions from Gandhi, the reformers stood opposite the police barrier in an attitude of prayer. They organized themselves into shifts, taking turns in standing there for six hours at a time. They built a hut nearby, undertook their duties on a religious basis and did hand-spinning while not on active duty. At no time did they use violence.

This program continued for months. Gandhi told them it must continue indefinitely until the hearts of the Brahmans were melted. When the rainy season came, the road, being on low ground, was flooded. Still the volunteers continued to stand, at times up to their shoulders in water, while the police kept up the cordon in small boats. The shifts had to be shortened to three hours.

The endurance and the consistent nonviolence of the reformers was finally too much for the Brahmans. In the autumn of 1925, after a year and four months, their obstinacy broke down, and they said, "We cannot any longer resist the prayers that have been made to us, and we are ready to receive the untouchables." The Brahmans opened the road to all comers and the low-caste people were allowed to walk at any time past the temple and past the Brahman quarters.

This change of policy had reverberations all through India and aided in removing similar restrictions against "untouchables" in other parts of India, and in strengthening the cause of caste reform.[4]

INDIA: KOTGARH

IN THE HIMALAYAS, north of Simla, there is a little district called Kotgarh, with a population of only a few thousand. This district is on the highway between India and Tibet. As the scenery is of surpassing beauty and grandeur and some good hunting ground is not far beyond, the road was frequented by hunters and government officials on vacations. Here, in 1921, another nonviolent struggle for economic justice was won.

For years there had been a custom known as *Begar,* whereby any government official or European could demand from any village headman along the road the services of as many men as the traveler desired, at any time, for as long a period as he wanted, for carrying luggage or messages at an utterly inadequate wage. Also the people could be required to drive their cows to the dak bungalow (a sort of inn) and supply as much milk as the traveler desired, also at ridiculously low prices. Thus farmers, many more than were needed, could be haled away from plowing, or sowing or harvesting their crops or any other pressing business, to suit the whims of any European who was on the road.

One of the local Indian leaders protested, but he was immediately jailed and the villagers were threatened with talk of machine guns and the like. An ex-American resident of the district, S. E. Stokes, decided to organize the resistance against this injustice. He was in sympathy with Gandhi's ideas and worked out the plan on nonviolent lines. Gandhi himself had no part in the struggle.

The district elected a small committee or *panchayat* to direct the movement, of which Stokes was a leading member. In every village in the district all the people took an oath by their village gods to obey the orders of the committee and not to negotiate with the government in this matter except through the committee.

The committee wrote out a long and carefully worded statement of the situation and its injustices and sent it to the district commissioner. They requested hearings, but no notice was taken of it by the commissioner. Letters were written to all the responsible officials. Copies of all letters were retained by the committee. Still the *Begar* exactions continued. The committee then notified the commissioner that if the exactions were not ended on a stated date the entire district would refuse all requests for service.

This brought action. The commissioner came up from Simla and called a large meeting. He threatened and used every stratagem he could to cause division between the different villages and castes, so as to break down the authority of the committee. But every man who was asked a question declined to answer except through the committee. Moreover, they all refused to give food or any service to any government official or European traveling on that part of the road.

In a few weeks the district commissioner had acceded to every single demand of the villagers' committee, and had to post all along the road printed rules which strictly limited the amount of service that could be asked and specified the wages. The struggle lasted several months, without the least violence by the farmers, and the outcome was a complete success in the district.[5]

INDIA: BARDOLI

IN BARDOLI TALUKA, a small district near Surat in Bombay Presidency, 88,000 peasants undertook a nonviolent campaign in 1928 to correct an economic injustice.

Contrary to the advice of the Joint Parliamentary Committee appointed to consider the Government of India Bill, 1919, and contrary to a resolution of the Legislative Council of the Bombay Presidency in 1924, the Bombay Provincial Government in 1927 raised the rate of rural taxation very severely—nominally 22 percent but in actual application in some instances over 60 percent. The peasantry claimed that the investigation upon which the increase had been based was wholly inadequate, that the tax official's report was inaccurate and carelessly compiled, and that the increase was unwarranted and unjust. They asked the governor to appoint an independent and impartial committee of inquiry to hold a thorough public investigation of all the evidence. The government paid no attention to the request. Then, after giving due notice of their intentions, the peasants of the entire district refused to pay the tax.

At the initiative and request of the local people, the movement was led by Vallabhbhai Patel, with the inspiration and advice of Gandhi. Patel held several large conferences with representatives from more than half the villages and of every class and religious community. He questioned these representatives very closely to estimate their determination and strength, and the cohesion and staying power of each and every village of the entire district. He explained in detail the history of the case, their legal rights and the justice of their demands. He described clearly and fully to the villagers the possibilities and terrors of government power. He told them that the struggle might be prolonged indefinitely. He gave them several days to think it all over, to count the cost, and to discuss it among themselves. Later, they returned to a still larger meeting and after further discussion resolved to enter upon the struggle.

For several years there had been four or five social service centers in different parts of the district, headed by well-trained and disciplined workers. These were the beginning of the organization. Sixteen "camps" were located at convenient places through the district, and about 250 volunteer leaders were placed in these camps. In addition, there were volunteers in each village. These volunteers were to collect the news and information about the struggle in each village and forward it promptly every day to the headquarters of the movement. The volunteers also kept careful watch of the movements of all government officials and warned the people of their coming and intentions. A news bulletin was printed every day and distributed to every village. Eventually, 10,000 copies a day were distributed in the district and 4,000 to subscribers outside. Patel's speeches were also distributed in pamphlet form. For the first month the volunteers spent much time getting signatures to a printed pledge in which the signers promised to stick together under their leaders, to adhere to truth and to remain nonviolent no matter what happened. Almost everyone signed the pledge. The women were organized as well as the men and took just as active a part.

The government did its best to compel the peasants to pay the tax. It tried flattery and bribery with some; fines, floggings and imprisonment of others. It tried to divide the communities against each other. The government officers seized and sold goods of the peasantry. It caused much of the peasants' land to be forfeited, and sold over 1,400 acres of such land at auction. It brought in numbers of Pathans, Moslems of the Northwest Frontier Province, who insulted and tried to terrorize the villagers, who were mostly Hindus. There were but few waverers or weaklings. The oppression solidified the feeling of the people. A strong social boycott was maintained against all government representatives and any one who purchased distrained goods or forfeited lands. The boycott did not interfere with the supply of physical necessities to such people.

The publicity all over the country was enormous, and the sympathy of Indians of all kinds was almost universally with the peasants. The matter was discussed very fully in the provincial legislature, and several members of the legislature resigned in protest against the government's stand. The matter was discussed even in Parliament in London.

Through it all, the peasants stood firm and nonviolent. After five and a half months, the government had to yield to practically every one of the demands. The governor appointed a committee of inquiry, agreed to restore all the land that had been sold or forfeited, and reinstated the village officials who had resigned. When the committee of inquiry made its report, it "substantially justified" the original complaints of the peasants and recommended a tax increase less than that which had been assessed by the government.[6]

INDIA: THE STRUGGLE FOR INDEPENDENCE

OTHER INSTANCES of the successful use of organized mass nonviolent resistance include the Ahmedabad mill strike in 1917 and the struggles against the government at Kheda in 1916-17 and at Borsad in 1923 against unjust taxes, and at Nagpur in 1927 for the right to parade with an Indian Nationalist flag. All of these were conducted or supervised by Gandhi.

Besides these there was the all-India non-cooperation struggle of 1921-22 which was unsuccessful in its immediate objective and yet immensely successful in awakening that country with its population of 350,000,000 people to desire freedom and to work concretely for its attainment. It profoundly altered the entire political situation in India, and thereby in the British Empire.[7] Here are portions of press dispatches about two incidents in the continuing struggle of 1930.[8]

The *New York Telegram* carried a long dispatch from Webb Miller, special correspondent for the United Press. I quote only a part:

"Dharasana Camp, Surat District, Bombay Presidency, May 22 (by mail)—Amazing scenes were witnessed yesterday when more than 2,500 Gandhi 'volunteers' advanced against the salt pans here in defiance of police regulations.

"The official government version of the raid, issued today, stated that 'from

Congress sources it is estimated 170 sustained injuries, but only three or four were seriously hurt.'

"About noon yesterday I visited the temporary hospital in the Congress camp and counted more than 200 injured lying in rows on the ground. I verified by personal observation that they were suffering injuries. Today even the British owned newspapers give the total number at 320. . . .

"The scene at Dharasana during the raid was astonishing and baffling to the Western mind accustomed to see violence met by violence, to expect a blow to be returned and a fight result. During the morning I saw and heard hundreds of blows inflicted by the police, but saw not a single blow returned by the volunteers. So far as I could observe the volunteers implicitly obeyed Gandhi's creed of non-violence. In no case did I see a volunteer even raise an arm to deflect the blows from lathis. There were no outcries from the beaten Swarajists, only groans after they had submitted to their beating.

"Obviously it was the purpose of the volunteers to force the police to beat them. The police were placed in a difficult position by the refusal to disperse and the action of volunteers in continually pressing closer to the salt pans.

"Many times I saw the police vainly threaten the advancing volunteers with upraised lathis. Upon their determined refusal to recede the lathis would fall upon the unresisting body, the volunteer would fall back bleeding or bruised and be carried away on a stretcher. Waiting volunteers, on the outskirts of the pans, often rushed and congratulated the beaten volunteer as he was carried off the field. It was apparent that most of the injured gloried in their injuries. One leader was heard to say, 'These men have done a great work for India today. They are martyrs to the cause.'

"Much of the time the stolid native Surat police seemed reluctant to strike. It was noticeable that when the officers were occupied on other parts of the line the police slackened, only to resume threatening and beating when the officers appeared again. I saw many instances of the volunteers pleading with the police to join them.

"At other times the police became angered, whereupon the beating would be done earnestly. During several of these incidents I saw the native police deliberately kick lying or sitting volunteers who refused to disperse. And I saw several instances where the police viciously jabbed sitting volunteers in the abdomen with the butt end of their lathi. . . .

"Once I saw a native policeman in anger strike a half-submerged volunteer who had already been struck down into a ditch and was clinging to the edge of the bank. This incident caused great excitement among the volunteers who witnessed it.

"My reaction to the scenes was of revulsion akin to the emotion one feels when seeing a dumb animal beaten—partly anger, partly humiliation. It was to the description of these reactions that the Bombay censorship authorities objected among other things.

"In fairness to the authorities it must be emphasized that the Congress volunteers were breaking laws or attempting to break them, and that they repeatedly refused to disperse and attempted to pull down the entanglements with ropes, and that the volunteers seemed to glory in their injuries.

"In eighteen years of reporting in twenty-two countries, during which I have witnessed innumerable civil disturbances, riots, street fights and rebellions, I have never witnessed such harrowing scenes as at Dharasana. The Western mind can grasp violence returned by violence, can understand a fight, but is,

I found, perplexed and baffled by the sight of men advancing coldly and deliberately and submitting to beating without attempting defense. Sometimes the scenes were so painful that I had to turn away momentarily.

"One surprising feature was the discipline of the volunteers. It seemed they were thoroughly imbued with Gandhi's nonviolence creed, and the leaders constantly stood in front of the ranks imploring them to remember that Gandhi's soul was with them."

The Chicago *Daily News* published the following account from Negley Farson, its special correspondent in India:

"Bombay, June 21.—Heroic, bearded Sikhs, several with blood dripping from their mouths, refusing to move or even to draw their 'kirpans' (sacred swords) to defend themselves from the shower of lathi blows—

"Hindu women and girls dressed in orange robes of sacrifice, flinging themselves on the bridles of horses and imploring mounted police not to strike male Congress volunteers, as they were Hindus themselves—

"Stretcher bearers waiting beside little islands of prostrate unflinching, immovable Satyagrahis, who had flung themselves on the ground grouped about their women upholding the flag of Swaraj—

"These were the scenes on the Maidan Esplanade, Bombay's splendid seafront park, where the six-day deadlock between police and Mahatma Gandhi's followers has broken out in a bewildering brutal and stupid yet heroic spectacle.

"The scene opened at six o'clock outside the Esplanade. At the police station facing the park some hundreds of yellow turbaned blue-clad, bare-legged Mahratti policemen were leaning on their dreaded bamboo lathis under the command of a score of English police sergeants in topees and cotton drill.

"At 6:45, marching in good formation down the tree-lined pleasant boulevard, came the first detachment of volunteers. This was the ambulance unit, mostly boys and young doctors, dressed in khaki with Red Cross badges on their arms. They marched past the waiting police without a glance to the south side of the playing field, where they parked their ambulances and brought out their stretchers.

"It was like nurses and orderlies preparing an operating theater.

"At 7 o'clock began to come processions of white-robed volunteers bearing red, green and white banners, singing 'We will take Swaraj—India Our Motherland.' At the head of each walked a tiny detachment of women and girls dressed in orange robes, many garlanded with jasmine. They marched steadily on past the policemen and actually lined up behind the stretchers.

"They waited there in a long front down the boulevard for the order to march on the field.

"I shall not forget the scenes which followed. Darkfaced Mahratti policemen in their yellow turbans marched along in column led by English sergeants across the field toward the waiting crowd. As they neared it the police went faster and faster. The Hindus, who may be willing to die but dread physical pain, watched them approach with frightened eyes. Then the police broke into a charge.

"Many Hindus at once ran, fleeing down the streets—but most stood stock still.

"Crash! Whack! Whack! Whack! At last the crowd broke. Only the orange clad women were left standing beside the prostrate figures of crumpled men. Congress volunteer ambulances clanging bells, stretcher bearers running hel-ter-skelter across the field. Whack! Whack! Whack!

"A minute's lull and then, with flags flying another column of volunteers marched onto the vast green field. A column of Mahrattas marched to meet them. They clashed—a clash, a rattle, dull thuds, then the faint-hearted ran and again there was the spectacle of the green field dotted with a line of fallen bodies and again the same islands of orange clad Hindu women holding up the flags of Swaraj.

"And here in the center of one of these islands sat a little knot of men, their heads bowed, submitting to a rain of lathi blows—refusing to move until on a stretcher and completely laid out. And there were stretchers within two feet of the suffering men, waiting for them.

"Then came a band of fifty Sikhs—and a heroic scene. The Sikhs, as you know, are a fierce fighting brotherhood. As soon as he can raise one, every man wears a beard which he curls around a cord or ties to his ears. The Sikhs also wear their hair long like women and curl it in a topknot under their turbans. These Sikhs were Akalis of a fanatic religious sect. They wore the kirpan, or sacred sword.

"With them were fifteen of their young girls and women. The women also wore sacred swords, and although dressed in orange saris like Hindu women, they wore little cotton trousers which reached to their tiny, sandaled feet. They were pretty girls and not so loud voiced and excited as the Hindu ladies. They simply smiled—as if they liked danger—which they do.

"One of them had her little baby, which she wanted to hold up before the police to dare them to come on. She laughed at me when my remark was translated that it was terrible to drag a child into this.

"Coming from all districts as representatives of the fighting Punjab, these Sikhs swore they would not draw their kirpans to defend themselves, but they would not leave the field. They did not.

" 'Never, never, never!' they cried, to the terrific delight of their Hindu brothers, in Swaraj. 'We will never retreat. We will die, we will!' The police hesitated before hitting the Sikhs. They asked their women would they not please, please, leave the field.

" 'No!' said the women, 'we will die with our men.'

"Mounted Indian policemen who had been galloping across the field, whacking heads indiscriminately, came to a stymie when they faced the little cluster of blue Akali turbans on the slender Sikh men.

" 'The Sikhs are brave men—how can we hit them?' It was not fear, but respect.

"But the police, determined to try to clear the field, at last rushed around the Shikh women and began to hit the men. I stood within five feet of a Sikh leader as he took the lathi blows. He was a short, heavily muscled man.

"The blows came—he stood straight. His turban was knocked off. The long black hair was bared with the round topknot. He closed his eyes as the blows fell—until at last he swayed and fell to the ground.

"No other Sikhs had tried to shield him, but now, shouting their defiance, they wiped away the blood streaming from his mouth. Hysterical Hindus rushed to him, bearing cakes of ice to rub the contusions over his eyes. The Sikh gave me a smile—and stood for more.

"And then the police threw up their hands. 'You can't go on hitting a blighter when he stands up to you like that.'"

In 1947, after twenty-six years of nonviolent struggle under Gandhi's leadership, India won her political freedom from Britain. Not a single Briton, so far as I know, was killed by Indians as part of this struggle. It was the Indians who voluntarily endured the necessary deaths and suffering. This was the first time in the history of the world that a great empire had been persuaded by nonviolent resistance to grant freedom to one of its subject countries. Of course, as in all great and complex events, there were many reasons for the result, but the nonviolent method is what eventually unified all Indians and gave them the necessary self-respect, self-reliance, courage and persistence, and also resulted in mutual respect and good feeling between Great Britain and India at the end.

IN OTHER COUNTRIES there have been instances of the successful use of this method. Here are the stories of three of them.

DENMARK

THE NAZIS INVADED Denmark in April 1940, giving the Danish King and Prime Minister only one hour to choose between admitting German troops without fighting or having the Danish cities bombed like Rotterdam. The King and Prime Minister, within the hour, issued a proclamation calling on the army and Danish people not to fight. The Nazis, eager to win converts to the New Order and probably wanting to use Danish agriculture to the utmost and save their troops for attacks elsewhere, pledged that they would not in any way interfere with Denmark's constitutional guarantees of civil liberties or with the workers' or farmers' organizations.

The German government issued strict orders to its soldiers to behave with the utmost "correctness" toward the Danes; the coalition cabinet under Social Democratic leadership was permitted to function, and an effort was made by the Nazis to convert Denmark into a "show window" for the New Order. From the first of the invasion the King, in order to encourage the people, rode on horseback every day through the streets of the capital city. Though at first the Nazis interfered relatively little with Danish domestic policy, gradually they began to put pressure on the Danes to conform with the Nazi program.

Late in 1940 the Nazis displayed the swastika emblem from a Danish public building. According to a report in *The New York Times,* "the monarch protested that the act was contrary to the occupation agreement and demanded that the flag be removed. The German military officials refused. 'I will send a soldier to remove it,' the king replied, or so the story ran. He was informed the soldier would be shot. 'I am the soldier,' he retorted, and the Nazi flag was lowered."[9]

The Nazis compelled the Danish Prime Minister, Scavenius, to sign the *Anti-Comintern* Pact without consultation with his cabinet colleagues or with King Christian. But the Danish Government flatly disavowed the pact.

The German efforts to win over the Danish people were unsuccessful. Danish response to German offers of friendship was the "cold shoulder." While large-scale sabotage was discouraged by the Danish authorities, the Danes used the slow-down and other similar tactics whenever possible against the Nazis.

When the Germans tried to compel the Danes to adopt the Nürnberg laws against the Jews, the Danes refused. When the Germans ordered that all Danish Jews should wear a yellow star and that a Jewish ghetto should be established, King Christian announced that if this were done he would be pleased to move from his palace to such a ghetto and, according to an Associated Press dispatch of October 11, 1942, said, "If the Germans want to put the yellow Jewish star in Denmark, I and my whole family will wear it as a sign of the highest distinction." He attended in full uniform a special celebration in a Copenhagen synagogue. All over Denmark opposition to the German plans of repression arose. Pastoral letters were issued by the Bishop of Zealand and others, protesting in the name of Christianity against the introduction of humiliating anti-Jewish measures.

In a Danish parliamentary by-election held in March 1943, the vote was 95 percent against the Nazis.

From June to September 1942, the King was sick with jaundice, and in October, while riding in the streets, he was thrown from his horse and received severe head injuries. Then he got pneumonia. Thus the people were deprived of their great leader till May 1943.

Among the people, resistance to the Nazis increased, especially in the form of sabotage. In May 1943, the King warned the people against the growing sabotage in munition works and railways. The

British Government had secretly been instigating the Danes to more sabotage and violence. In August 1943, fighting broke out between German soldiers and Danish civilians, especially in Odensee, the third-largest city in the country; there was a four-day general strike at Esbjerg; the Danes scuttled one of the ships of their navy, and other Danish naval units fled to Sweden.

The Germans placed King Christian and his family under house arrest and poured troops into the country, and several thousand Danes were killed.

All this time the Danes, at great risk to themselves, had been sheltering Jews and smuggling them to Sweden in spite of the German ships patrolling the intervening seas.

Even while under house arrest, the King refused to form a pro-Nazi government. He was quoted by a Danish refugee as having requested the Danish Bishop Fugelsang Damgaard to "tell everyone that peace is on its way. We have allies in other countries fighting for our cause. Let everyone know that so long as the Germans are in the country I will sign no decree forming a new Danish government. What I have signed so far has been forced. God protect you all. God protect our country."[10]

Thus the Danes, without previous preparation or training in nonviolent resistance, nevertheless used this kind of defense, not perfectly, yet effectively, against the ruthless Nazis whose cruelty and iron discipline was a byword. The Danes resisted nonviolently and successfully for two and a half years, until the warring British government persuaded them to use violence.

NORWAY

DENMARK'S NEIGHBOR, Norway, was invaded by the Nazis in April 1940. For two months the Norwegians offered armed resistance which was wholly suppressed by the far more powerful Nazi troops. A pro-German Norwegian, Vidkun Quisling, was made dictator of the country by the Germans. The Norwegian king and government fled to London, leaving the people leaderless. The people wanted to resist but did not see how they could do so. Until September of that year there was confusion among the people. In the autumn some underground newspapers were started and distributed secretly.

The pressure and violence of the Nazis generated resistance. Spontaneously and without organization, school children and others began wearing paper clips as a sign of unity. The authorities sensed the meaning and forbade this action. Then people began wearing other emblems—coins, flowers on the King's birthday, red caps, even potatoes. Secret organizations grew up with headquarters at Oslo.

The first organized resistance came from the hundreds of thousands of youth in the athletic clubs. As soon as the Nazis tried to take control of these clubs, all organized activity immediately ceased and remained in abeyance till the Nazis left. Next to resist was the Supreme Court of Justice. As soon as the Germans tried to reshape the laws in accordance with Nazi principles, all the members of the Supreme Court resigned. The teachers and clergy especially embodied, upheld and stimulated the spirit of resistance. No leaders were chosen in advance; the resistance struggle produced its own leaders.

Gradually the resistance took form. Haaken Holmboe, a teacher in a small town north of Oslo, had heard of Gandhi and read a little about him. But very few others knew of Gandhi or the method of the Indian struggle for freedom. Holmboe became a contact point for resisters in a large rural district in East Norway in the autumn of 1941. During that autumn an underground press was started and maintained all through the five years of the German occupation. By this means the people were informed of what was happening and what they should do to resist. Imprisonment, torture and killing by the Nazis only made the resistance firmer and more complete.

In June 1941, Quisling abolished the former teachers' organization. His government was trying in various small ways to influence people to adopt Nazi ideology, such as by decreeing that Quisling's portrait should be hung in all schools. These efforts aroused strong opposition among both students and teachers. In February 1942, Quisling tried to start a corporate state on Mussolini's model. He began with the teaching profession. After the abolition of the former teachers' organization, a new teachers' organization was started with the chief of Quisling's secret police as its head. A new youth movement was set up by the government, also, modeled after the Nazi youth movement of Germany. The government decreed compulsory membership in it for all young people 10 to 18 years of age.

A secret illegal organization among the teachers had been developing. Its members decided that teachers would resist all the following four points: (1) any Government demand that teachers should become members of Quisling's party, the *Nasjonal Samling;* (2) any attempt to introduce *Nasjonal Samling* propaganda in the schools; (3) any order from outside the school authorities; (4) any collaboration with the *Nasjonal Samling* youth movement.

On February 20, 1942, between 8,000 and 10,000 of the total of 12,000 Norwegian teachers each wrote to Quisling's Education Department a declaration reading, "I declare that I cannot take part in the education of the youth of Norway along those lines which have been outlined for the *Nasjonal Samling* Youth Service, this being against my conscience. According to what the leader of the new teachers' organization has said, membership in this organization will mean an obligation for me to assist in such education, and would also force me to do other acts which are in conflict with the obligations of my profession. I find that I must declare that I cannot regard myself as a member of the new teachers' organization."

Every teacher wrote this statement himself, signed it with his own name, and mailed it himself to the Education Department of Quisling's government. On February 24, the Bishops of the State Church, who had already protested about the *Nasjonal Samling* Youth Service, resigned their official posts but retained their religious duties. On the same day, 150 University professors also protested against the *Nasjonal Samling* youth front.

On February 25, the Quisling government announced that the teachers' protests would be regarded as official resignations and that if they persisted they would be discharged. On the same day the Education Department closed all schools for a month, on the pretext of a shortage of fuel. From all over the country offers of fuel came to keep the schools open. The official newspapers told nothing about the teachers' resistance, but the "fuel holiday" spread the news.

On March 7, the official newspapers announced that 300 teachers would be called to do "some kind of social work in the north of Norway." In a bulletin of the Education Department issued only to teachers, March 15 was set as the final date for compliance; teachers who resisted government orders after that date were threatened with loss of jobs, pay and pensions. The Quisling Education Department received tens of thousands of letters of protest from nearly ten percent of Norway's parents.

When March 15 came, the teachers remained defiant. None of them crumbled. Beginning about March 20, about one thousand men teachers were arrested, among them Haaken Holmboe, but no women teachers. The arrests did not terrify the people. Arrests seemed to be haphazard. Neither all the leaders nor all the weaklings were arrested. After the arrests, the clergy made a statement in the churches at Easter, and nearly all of them resigned their jobs. Many of the clergy were transferred to other places than their homes; their leaders were sent to prison and concentration camps.

From southern and western Norway about 650 of the arrested teachers were transferred from jails to a concentration camp at Grini. From some undisclosed source—not the government—their families received the equivalent of their salaries all through their detention. In the camp the government issued an ultimatum to the imprisoned teachers, but only three gave in.

On March 31, the 650 teachers were taken in cattle cars to another concentration camp about two hundred kilometers from Oslo. At the railway stations, children gathered and sang to them as the train passed through. A few more were added, making their total number 687. After a few days at the new camp they were put on rations of four small slices of bread (150 grams) a day and water. The bread was given out at night. Each morning they were compelled to crawl and run in deep snow for an hour and a half. Then came an hour and a half of heavy work, mostly shoveling snow, followed by another hour and a half of crawling and running in the snow. Then they were given a meal of hot water. After the second day of this, seventy-six of the older teachers, from 55 to 59 years of age, were questioned by camp officials, but not a single one of them backed down.

In most places elsewhere in Norway, the government reopened the schools on April 8 except in Oslo and Aker, and even there the schools reopened a few days later. But in reporting for work, all the teachers publicly repudiated membership in Quisling's new teacher organization and told their classes so the first day. The teachers spoke to the children of conscience, of the spirit of truth and of their responsibility to the children. Among the teachers there was a strong feeling of solidarity.

Among the imprisoned teachers two cases of pneumonia developed.

When another of the teachers physically collapsed and a German officer asked him why he did not give in, the teacher answered, "Because I am a Norwegian." After several days more of this treatment, the camp authorities marched the prisoners through a room, asking each one if he would sign a retraction of his protest. As they filed through the room each prisoner said "No," often in advance of the officer's question. Out of 637 prisoner teachers only 32, after this grueling treatment, retracted. So the terrorism and torture gymnastics were resumed, and the starvation rations continued. All the time, threatening rumors were circulated among the teachers, both inside and outside of the camp. Yet the wives of the teachers said they did not want their husbands to yield, and sent that word to them.

After about a week of this treatment, 499 of them were taken in cattle cars to Trondheim and thence in a steamer built to carry only 100 passengers, north for thirteen days to Kirkenes, a small town near the Finnish (now Russian) border, far beyond the Arctic Circle. There, custody of them was transferred from the German *Gestapo* to the *Wehrmacht*. In a few days more the remaining 153 teachers, after again refusing to give in, were also sent to Kirkenes.

When the schools at Oslo reopened on May 7, the teachers there also dissociated themselves from the new government-sponsored teachers' organization.

At Kirkenes there were no beds, bedding, mattresses or furniture for the teachers. Surreptitiously they got hay from nearby haystacks. The prisoners were put to work unloading from ships heavy crates of supplies and oil drums. Though they had not been trained for such work, they worked seven days a week. One was killed, two lost an eye each, and one broke a leg and both arms.

The deportation of the teachers to Kirkenes stiffened the morale and resistance of the other people of Norway enormously. Quisling knew that if he became harsher with the teachers, the resistance of the rest of the country would become far stronger and more difficult to deal with. Talking to a group of teachers in a small town on March 22, Quisling threatened, stormed and raged at them. He ended by saying, "You teachers have destroyed everything for me." He had them all arrested. Next day a few teachers of that school who had been absent when he spoke went to the hall and asked to be imprisoned with the others. Quisling had intended the new organization of teachers to be the pilot project of his corporate state, but the teachers blocked it.

In late August, 50 teachers who were ill were sent home. On September 16, a second group of about 100 were sent back home. On November 4, the remaining 400 or so were sent home from the camp, after eight months of hard forced labor. They were allowed to remain teaching without recanting their principles.

All this nonviolent resistance was unprepared for. There was no training. It grew up out of the strong urge to resist *somehow*. There was no theory or philosophy in it. Most of the people would have used violence if they had had the means. Toward the end there was a secret military organization called *Milarg,* promoted and supplied by the British. But most of the resistance, which lasted five years, was nonviolent.

President Franklin D. Roosevelt is reported to have said on September 16, 1942, "If there is anyone who doubts the democratic will to win . . . let him look to Norway. . . . Norway at once conquered and unconquerable. At home the Norwegian people have silently resisted the invader's will with grim endurance."[11]

This Norwegian nonviolent resistance was possible because all the people were self-respecting, self-reliant, self-confident, courageous, filled with a spirit of unity, independence and liberty, and felt urgently and steadily that they had to resist somehow. It was unpremeditated and spontaneous.

Of the forms it took, one of the leaders, Diderich Lund, wrote afterward that the Norwegian economic resistance broke down completely. Sabotage was effective only to a small degree, and secrecy was also not as effective as bold, forthright candor and adherence to open truth. Those who resisted in this spirit were filled with a "strange feeling of quiet happiness . . . even under hard and difficult conditions," says Lund. "The unshakable conviction of fighting in a good cause has always been the strongest incitement to the making of fanatical soldiers, and perhaps we also need fanatics. But above all we need efficiency and wisdom, courage and readiness to self-sacrifice. If we possess to some degree these qualities, nonviolent resistance will give us the sure and joyful knowledge of fighting in the cause of justice and love. And we shall also know that our fight is the only one leading to lasting victory."[12]

UNITED STATES: MONTGOMERY

THROUGHOUT THE Southern states of the United States, custom and state laws have combined to segregate Negroes from whites in respect to hotels, restaurants, schools, housing, use of parks and recreation grounds, waiting rooms in railway stations, on trains, buses, street cars and all sorts of public facilities. In many localities in such states, Negroes were not and are still not allowed to vote. Until fairly recently, white mobs would occasionally lynch a Negro without even the pretense of a trial. Often Negroes would be arrested and punished for alleged misdemeanors, the real reason being to assert the superior status and power of the white man. All this is the result of the fact that Negroes were formerly slaves of the white man and considerably outnumber the whites in some parts of those states. The white man's idea of his own superiority has been unyielding.

Very slowly after 1870, but increasingly in recent decades, Negroes have been gradually getting more and better education and rising economically. During the First World War Negro regiments made a good record. They were asked and compelled to suffer and die for the white man's civilization. In the Second World War Negroes were integrated with whites in the same companies and regiments and were admitted as pilots in the Air Force, and again did splendidly. But after the war, when they came back to civilian life, they were treated again as second-class citizens. Naturally they did not care to be considered cannon fodder, and naturally they keenly resented such indignities, but the majority of Negroes were discouraged and unwilling to assert their rights. In 1954, however, the United States Supreme Court decided that segregation in public schools was unconstitutional and would have to stop, though it allowed a certain gradualness for the change.

In Montgomery, Alabama, the "cradle of the Confederacy," racial segregation of course prevailed. In the buses, the first four rows of seats from the front, holding about ten persons, were reserved for whites, and theoretically the last three rows of seats were reserved for Negroes. But if a white person boarded the bus when the front four rows were filled with whites and the last rows filled with Negroes, the bus driver would ask a Negro to "move back" and he would have to stand while the white person took his seat. Sometimes this request was made courteously, but often rudely and insultingly.

On December 1, 1955, a Negro seamstress, Mrs. Rosa Parks, boarded a bus to get home after her day's work. She sat down in the first seat behind the section reserved for whites. Soon after she took her seat, some white people got on the bus and the driver ordered Mrs. Parks and three other Negroes on that seat to move back in order to accommodate the whites. By that time all the other seats were occupied. The other three Negroes complied with the order. Mrs. Parks quietly refused. The driver called the police and she was arrested for violating the city's segregation ordinance.

She was a quiet, dignified person, with a sweet personality, soft-spoken and calm in all situations, and highly respected in the Negro community. She could no longer endure the indignities to which she and other Negroes had been subjected. Her self-respect could take it no more.

This arrest proved to be a trigger which released the long-smouldering resentment of the Negro community into action. A few Negro leaders, including E. D. Nixon, head of the local union of sleeping-car porters, and a number of Negro ministers agreed that a boycott of all the buses by all the Negroes should be undertaken as a protest. A meeting of Negro leaders of almost all groups in the community was called and they decided that the whole Negro community of Montgomery should be asked to boycott the buses all day Monday, December 5, and then come to a mass meeting in one of the Negro churches that evening to decide what further action to take. The Negro ministers agreed to tell their congregations on Sunday. From the beginning, the Negro ministers played a very large part in the leadership of the protest. The newspapers got hold of the story and published it and thus spread the news all through the Negro community.

The boycott was a complete success. Not one of the fifty thousand Negroes of the city rode that day in a bus. That same day Mrs. Parks was tried in court and fined ten dollars. She appealed from the decision to a higher court. The mass meeting that night filled the church to overflowing, two and a half hours before the time set for it. Those present decided unanimously to continue the boycott until: (1) courteous treatment by the bus operators was guaranteed; (2) passengers were seated on a first-come, first-served basis—Negroes seating from the back of the bus toward the front while whites seated from the front toward the back; (3) Negro bus operators were employed on predominantly Negro routes. They formed an organization to direct the protest, and named it the Montgomery Improvement Association. They chose as president of it a young, highly educated Negro minister, Martin Luther King Jr., who had pondered social problems earnestly and been much influenced by Thoreau's "Essay on Civil Disobedience" and the teaching and program of Mahatma Gandhi. Most of the other leaders of the MIA were ministers, too, and all were Negroes, except Robert Graetz, white minister of a Negro church, the only white minister in the whole city who took part in or showed sympathy toward the protest.

The leaders promptly organized several committees: for transportation, finance and strategy, a program committee for the mass meetings, and an executive committee.

The transportation committee first organized a Negro taxi service, but this was blocked by an existing law which required a minimum fare of 45 cents for any taxi ride. Then a car-pool was formed and later was added to by station wagons bought and operated for this purpose by several of the Negro churches and by other contributors. Transportation under the car-pool was quickly and efficiently organized. Yet thousands of Negroes had to walk. Once a pool driver stopped beside an elderly Negro woman who was trudging with obvious difficulty. "Jump in, grandmother," he said, "you don't need to walk." She waved him to go on. "I'm not walking for myself," she called out, "I'm walking for my children and grandchildren." Another Negro woman said she preferred tired feet to a tired soul.

Mass meetings were held twice a week in the Negro churches, rotating from one to another. They were always crowded, frequently using loudspeakers for the people who could not get in. The programs included prayers, scripture readings, much singing of hymns, especially Negro spirituals, and reports by committees. Enthusiasm ran high. Dr. King and the other leaders explained the philosophy and methods of the movement night after night. It was a combination of Jesus' ethic of love and Gandhi's nonviolent resistance. Dr. King explained in great detail its effectiveness and applications, emphasizing the essential importance of love and nonviolence, no matter under what provocation. To make the method more vivid, they acted out possible situations where violence might be used against them, and how to behave under such circumstances.

The boycott was effective, complete and enduring. The city council tried to break it by having Negro car drivers arrested on all sorts of pretexts. The insurance companies were pressured into canceling the insurance on Negro cars. But this attack was defeated by getting car insurance from Lloyds of London. False rumors were spread that Negro leaders had agreed to call off the boycott, and a fake settlement was announced in the newspapers. Attempts were made to disrupt the unity of the Negro leaders by inciting jealousy. Dr. King was arrested and jailed for allegedly speeding in his car, but the crowd of Negroes who promptly gathered at the jail was so large, though entirely peaceful, that the jailer took fright and released him on his own bond. Then anonymous persons, members of the Ku Klux Klan and probably of the White Citizens' Council, segregationist organizations, began sending anonymous letters and telephone calls to the Negro leaders, especially Dr. King. On the night of January 30, 1956, a bomb was thrown on the porch of Dr. King's house. Luckily the property damage was slight and nobody was injured. A crowd of angry Negroes rapidly gathered, but Dr. King pleaded with them not to be violent or angry, and they obeyed him. Two nights later a bomb was thrown at the house of E. D. Nixon, another leader. But this violence only made the boycott firmer.

All these events were dramatic and the protest most unusual, especially in the South and yet more especially because of the complete, deliberate, disciplined, religiously motivated nonviolence of the Negroes. The news of it traveled all over the world. Although no public appeal for funds was made, contributions poured in from all over the world. Gifts ranged from one dollar to five thousand dollars. Negro and white churches in almost every city in the United States sent money. Labor, civic and social groups supported the movement. Almost every branch of the National Association for the Advancement of Colored People helped. A former federal judge wrote, "You have shown that decency and courage will ultimately prevail." From Singapore came a message, "What you are doing is a real inspiration to us here." A Swiss woman sent five hundred dollars and words of encouragement. The crew of a ship at sea cabled,

"We offer a prayer in sympathy in the fight for justice." From Pennsylvania came a check for one hundred dollars from an elderly lady, and a note saying, "Your work is outstanding and unprecedented in the history of our country. Indeed, it is epoch-making and it should have far-reaching effect. 'Not by might, nor by power, but by my spirit, saith the Lord'—this might well be the motto of the Montgomery Improvement Association."

A large number of the Negro leaders were indicted, arrested and tried for conspiracy to prevent the operation of a lawful business. Dr. King was tried first, found guilty and fined five hundred dollars. He appealed the case. The Negro lawyers then filed a suit in the United States Federal Court asking that bus segregation be stopped because it was contrary to the 14th Amendment to the U. S. Constitution. After about three weeks the Federal judges decided that the city bus segregation laws of Alabama were unconstitutional. The city appealed the case. So the boycott had to continue and did.

The city brought suit in November 1956 to enjoin the operation of the Negro car-pool. The petition was directed against the Montgomery Improvement Association and several Negro churches and individuals. During the trial, news came that the United States Supreme Court had affirmed the decision of the lower Federal Court that the Alabama state and local laws requiring segregation on buses were unconstitutional. The executive board of the Montgomery Improvement Association, on advice of counsel, decided to end the official protest immediately but to delay the return to the buses until the official mandatory order from the Supreme Court was received.

That night there was an enthusiastic meeting of eight thousand Negroes. Later in the evening the Ku Klux Klan paraded in the Negro section of the city, but this time the Negroes were not intimidated. In subsequent Negro mass meetings, the people were instructed to be completely nonviolent and conciliatory in manner and action when they began riding the buses again. Scenes of possible provocation were described, enacted and rehearsed in "socio-dramas" at these meetings. Constant courtesy and loving attitudes were enjoined. The Supreme Court's mandate was received on December 20, 1956, a little over a year after the beginning of the boycott. Except for a few minor incidents of white anger against Negroes, the resumption of riding by Negroes passed off smoothly. As far as possible, two

Negro ministers rode on each bus line in the city during the rush hours of the morning and afternoon of the first day, with the idea that their presence would give courage to the Negro citizens and make them less likely to retaliate in case of insults.

When Dr. King boarded the first morning bus, the bus driver greeted him with a cordial smile. As he put his fare in the box the driver said, "I believe you are Reverend King, aren't you?"

Dr. King replied, "Yes, I am."

"We are glad to have you this morning," said the driver. Newspaper reporters and television men were also on the same bus.

But within ten days, white violence began. City buses were fired upon. Negroes were assaulted. Four Negro churches were bombed and also two Negro ministers' houses. Two of the churches were almost completely destroyed; the two others severely damaged. Luckily, no person was injured in the bombings.

This violence made the white leaders realize that such anarchy and violence were making the town unsafe for everybody and giving it a bad name in the country at large. The local newspaper published a strong editorial against it. The white man's business association publicly opposed the lawless violence. A number of white ministers denounced the bombing. Still there were more bombings. The city authorities offered a four-thousand-dollar reward for information leading to the arrest and conviction of the bombers. Seven white men were arrested and tried, but despite clear evidence of guilt the jury refused to convict them. The diehards had, however, made their last stand. The violence stopped abruptly. Desegregation on the buses proceeded smoothly.

So nonviolence, unity, forgiveness and love for enemies proved powerful. The racial problems of Montgomery are only beginning to be solved, but what Dr. King called a "stride toward freedom" had certainly been made.[13]

OTHER INSTANCES

IN ADDITION to the foregoing examples there were in the olden days in China extremely effective economic boycotts, nonviolent in outer form, against foreign goods. Soon after the First World War the coal miners of the Ruhr, in Germany, engaged in a predominately nonviolent strike and non-cooperation movement against the French government. It was so nearly successful that the victory of the French was really pyrrhic. In 1952 and again in 1957 in Johannesburg, South Africa, there were impressive nonviolent struggles by non-whites against the white-supremacist government. These were only two "battles" in what promises to be a long struggle. In March 1957, after a ten-year nonviolent struggle under the leadership of Kwame Nkrumah, what was formerly the British colony of the Gold Coast became the independent country of Ghana, in the British Commonwealth. Nkrumah knew of Gandhi and deliberately followed his method and advocates its use by all the African colonial peoples for attaining their freedom.

The principle of nonviolent resistance had been conceived and applied independently by numerous seers and courageous people in many different countries. Among them were Lao-tzü, Buddha, the Jain Tirthankaras, Jesus, St. Francis of Assisi, George Fox, Henry David Thoreau, Leo Tolstoi and many others too numerous to mention.[14] But Gandhi is the outstanding person in modern times who worked out the theory and applied it to mass movements in organized corporate fashion, and proved the validity of this extension by actual successful campaigns in numerous difficult situations. It seems probable that this method will be used increasingly in the coming years, especially since total war is now at stalemate because of nuclear and hydrogen bombs.

The method is adapted not merely to Oriental psychology and modes of thinking, feeling, acting and living. Its success does not depend on a value system shared by both parties to the struggle. Its record shows successful use by illiterate peasants and city-bred intellectuals, by saints and the ordinary run of mankind, rich men and poor, property owners and homeless vagabonds, women as well as men, by meat eaters and vegetarians, Europeans and Americans, Negroes and whites, Chinese and Indians, by the religious-minded and those not so accounted. It has been used successfully in political, economic and social conflicts, and against armed invasion by ruthless and highly disciplined troops. It has been used successfully by individuals and groups, both large and small.

Knowing that nonviolent resistance has actually been used with success, at least in certain instances, let us now try to understand how and why it works.

2

MORAL JIU-JITSU

MOST PEOPLE HITHERTO have been skeptical of nonviolent resistance simply because they did not understand how it could possibly work. They might be less skeptical once they could see how the method could operate and be effective. Let us then try to understand first how nonviolent resistance works. Later we may estimate the probabilities of its success in general use. Modern psychology enables us to understand the emotional, mental and moral mechanisms involved. So let us analyze the matter and pay attention to one part of the problem at a time. We will consider first its operation by individuals and later its use by organized groups of people.

If one man attacks another with physical violence and the victim hits back, the violent response gives the attacker a certain reassurance and moral support. It shows that the position of violence on the victim's scale of moral values is the same as that of the attacker. A mere display of either fear or anger by the victim is sufficient to have this effect. It makes the attacker sure of his own *savoir-faire*, of his choice of methods, of his knowledge of human nature and hence of his opponent. He can rely on the victim to react in a definite way. The attacker's morale is sustained, his sense of values is vindicated.

But suppose the assailant, using physical violence, attacks a different sort of person. The attitude of this new opponent is fearless, calm, steady; because of a different belief, training or experience he has much self-control. He does not respond to the attacker's violence with counter-violence. Instead, he accepts the blows good-temperedly, stating his belief as to the truth of the matter in dispute, asking for an examination of both sides of the dispute, and stating his readiness to abide by the truth. He offers resistance, but only in moral terms.

He states his readiness to prove his sincerity by his own suffering rather than by inflicting suffering on the assailant. He accepts blow after blow, showing no signs of fear or resentment, keeping steadily good-humored and kindly in look of eye, tone of voice, and posture of body and arms. To violence he opposes nonviolent resistance.

The assailant's first thought may be that his opponent is afraid of him, that he is a coward, ready to give way and acknowledge defeat. But the opponent's look and posture show not fear but courage. His steady resistance of will reveals no subservience. His unflinching endurance of pain is startling, particularly because, as F. C. Bartlett has pointed out, "it is easier and requires less courage to attack than to withstand fire without retaliation."[1]

At such an unusual and unexpected reaction the assailant will be surprised. If at first he was inclined to be scornful or contemptuous of the victim as a coward, those feelings rapidly become displaced by curiosity and wonder. As the psychologist Shand points out, "Wonder tends to exclude repugnance, disgust and contempt in relation to its object."[2]

Thus nonviolent resistance acts as a sort of moral jiu-jitsu. The nonviolence and good will of the victim act in the same way that the lack of physical opposition by the user of physical jiu-jitsu, does, causing the attacker to lose his moral balance. He suddenly and unexpectedly loses the moral support which the usual violent resistance of most victims would render him. He plunges forward, as it were, into a new world of values. He feels insecure because of the novelty of the situation and his ignorance of how to handle it. He loses his poise and self-confidence. The victim not only lets the attacker come, but, as it were, pulls him forward by kindness, generosity and voluntary suffering, so that the attacker loses his moral balance. The user of nonviolent resistance, knowing what he is doing and having a more creative purpose, keeps his moral balance. He uses the leverage of a superior wisdom to subdue the rough direct force of his opponent.[3]

Another way to state it is that between two persons in physically violent combat there may appear to be complete disagreement, but in reality they conduct their fight on the basis of a strong fundamental agreement that violence is a sound mode of procedure. Hence, if one of the parties eliminates that basic agreement, announcing by his actions that he has abandoned the method used by his ancestors almost as early as the beginning of animal life, it is no wonder that the other is startled and uncertain. His instincts no longer tell him instantly what to do. He feels that he has plunged into a new world.

Just as in jiu-jitsu, violence itself helps to overthrow its user. There are several reasons for this, besides the element of surprise.

First, prolonged anger is very exhausting. Undoubtedly anger at first gives an access of muscular and sometimes mental energy. But it also consumes energy very rapidly, and if long sustained it may completely exhaust the person feeling it.[4]

Second, part of the energy of the assailant is reverted and used up against himself. The steadfast appeals of an individual nonviolent resister work in the personality of the violent attacker, arousing the latter's more decent and kindly motives and putting them in conflict with his fighting, aggressive instincts. Thus the attacker's personality is divided. The appeals, like commercial advertising, may require considerable repetition before they become effective, but the result is pretty sure. They act on the principle of "summation of stimuli."[5]

The violent assailant realizes that he has made a mistake in thinking at first that his opponent was a coward. He is bothered by the thought that he may have made or might in future make another mistake about this unusual opponent, and that another mistake might be more embarrassing. He therefore becomes more cautious.

If there are onlookers, the assailant soon loses still more poise. Instinctively he dramatizes himself before them and becomes more aware of his position. With the audience as a sort of mirror, he realizes the contrast between his own conduct and that of the victim. In relation to the onlookers, the attacker with his violence perhaps begins to feel a little excessive and undignified—even a little ineffective—and by contrast with the victim, less generous and in fact brutal. He realizes that the onlookers see that he has misjudged the nature of his adversary, and realizes that he has lost prestige. He somewhat loses his inner self-respect, gets a sense of inferiority. Of course he does not want to acknowledge it, but his feelings betray themselves in hesitance of manner, speech or glance. The onlookers perceive it, and he himself senses a further loss of public support.

If anyone feels inclined to doubt such a reaction of the outsiders against the assailant's violence, let him recall what happens during a labor strike if any striker loses his temper and destroys property or attacks any person. Immediately the employers blazon the news in the press and try to make it appear that all the strikers are men of violence and that public safety is threatened. They play on the fears of the public and then persuade the authorities to call out extra police or soldiers. Public opinion, swayed by the press, reacts strongly against the strikers and their cause is lost. Violence which is not opposed by violence, but by courageous nonviolence, if it is in the open, is sure sooner or later to react against the attacker.

The disadvantage of the attacker increases by reason of a further loss of inner assurance. He becomes increasingly aware that the victim's scale of values is different from his own. He dimly realizes that the courage of the nonviolent opponent is higher than mere physical bravery or recklessness—that it is somehow a clearer and stronger realization of human nature or perhaps of some ultimate powers or realities in the background of life. He is surprised into an uncertainty of his own valuations and methods.

A final disadvantage and continuing cause of relative weakness in the attacker is that he is in a suggestible and receptive state of mind and emotion, more so than the nonviolent resister. The reasons for this are several. The emotion of the struggle of course tends to make both parties suggestible.[6] But the surprising conduct and attitude of the victim suddenly present a new idea to the attacker.[7] "The effect of surprise is to make us attend to the event that surprises us. Wonder tends to arrest and detain the attention on the thing which excites it."[8] The struggle is a process of mutual interacting influence. As this process proceeds, there is a cumulative effect of the several disabilities of the violent assailant as above described, together with advantages of the nonviolent opponent which we are about to set forth. This cumulative effect acts upon the subconscious and imagination of the attacker to keep him more suggestible than the nonviolent resister. Thus the assailant has less chance of influencing the resister than the latter has of influencing him.

In this moral jiu-jitsu, the nonviolent person has superior position, poise and power for many reasons. First, he has taken the moral initiative. His conduct is new, unexpected, and unpredictable to the person habituated to violence. Second, he is not surprised. He knows, by reasoning or by intuition and faith, what is really taking place in such a struggle, and how to control the process. Third, his self-control and lack of anger conserve his energy. Moreover, he is not in as suggestible a condition as his assailant.

He has still another element of superior power: he has demonstrated his sincerity and deep conviction. To be willing to suffer and die for a cause is an incontestable proof of sincere belief, and perhaps in most cases the only incontestable proof. Nonviolence coupled with voluntary suffering is just such an incontestable proof of sincerity. Voluntary suffering is probably also a sure sign that the whole being of the sufferer—body, mind, will and spirit—is integrated and at work with singleness of purpose. This means that immense and unpredictable resources of energy are in action and ready to endure. The sight and realization of this is profoundly impressive and moving.

Again, the victim's refusal to use violence indicates his respect for the personality and moral integrity of the assailant. From childhood we all tend to like people who show respect for our personality. This tendency operates even between the parties to a conflict. Such respect for the personality of the opponent was one of the important elements in the practice of medieval European chivalry, and added much to the charm and power of that code. Respect for personality is a prerequisite for real freedom and fine human association. It is proof of unselfishness and of moral poise and understanding. If, as at least two distinguished psychologists believe,* the self-regarding sentiment is the foundation of all the higher morality,[9] a demonstration of respect for personality exercises a much deeper and more far-reaching influence than is generally realized. This respect, shown by the nonviolent resister, gradually tends to put his attacker to shame and to enhance the respect of any onlookers toward the former.

Both opponents feel a desire and need for the approbation of others. Social approval and opprobrium are very strong forces. They act through and are a part of the herd or gregarious instinct that is so powerful in mankind.[10] The desire for outside approval is strikingly shown by the increasing emphasis on the uses of propaganda by major nations since World War I. Again, it is demonstrated in labor disputes in which both parties are at great pains to win public support and sympathy. All politicians recognize the force of public opinion.

For these reasons, in a struggle between a violent person and a non-

---

* William McDougal and A. G. Tansley.

violent resister, if there are any onlookers or a public that hears of the conflict, the nonviolent resister gains a strong advantage from their reaction. When the public sees the gentle person's courage and fortitude, notes his generosity and good will toward the attacker, and hears his repeated offers to settle the matter fairly, peaceably and openly, they are filled with surprise, curiosity and wonder. If they have been hostile to the victim before, they at least pause to think. His good humor, fairness and kindness arouse confidence. Sooner or later his conduct wins public sympathy, admiration and support, and also the respect of the violent opponent himself. Gandhi's chivalrous and generous conduct toward the South African government when it was threatened by a railway strike is an instance of this sort. Once the respect of the opponent has been secured, a long step has been taken toward a satisfactory solution of the controversy, no matter whether it be public or private.

But what is the psychology of the affair if the assailant is filled with the sort of cruelty or greed, pride, bigotry, or hardness that seems to grow on what it feeds on?

Cruelty is a complex of fear, anger and pride.[11] Greed is a distorted desire for security and completion. In a sense it is a fear of lack. Pride is another mistaken sense of divisiveness. Bigotry is an obstinate, narrow religious pride.

In all such instances, the tendency of nonviolent resistance is to remove fear, anger and any foreboding or dread of loss or sense of separateness (as will be seen in Chapter Five below), and to replace these with feelings of security, unity, sympathy and good will. Since fear and anger are elements of cruelty, the removal of fear and anger will tend to reduce cruelty. Shand tells us that "wonder tends to exclude repugnance, disgust and contempt in relation to its object."[12] Insofar as these may be elements involved in pride, the wonder evoked by the conduct of the nonviolent person also tends to reduce pride and hence to reduce cruelty. Insofar as cruelty is due to a desire for power or a feeling of superiority, the ability of nonviolence to win the support of the outside public presently makes the cruel person realize that the kind of power he has valued is disadvantageous and that perhaps he is not so superior as he had previously supposed.

Aside from its effect on the spectators, nonviolent resistance gradually creates even in the violent opponent himself a gradual realization of human unity and a different idea of what kind of power is desirable. Cruelty may be partly due to a defect in the cruel person's imagination or to dullness of observation, and in this event, dramatic scenes of prolonged nonviolent resistance act to stimulate his imagination and powers of observation, and thereby to reduce his cruelty. If avarice or desire for revenge are factors in a particular case of cruelty, these also are reduced by prolonged nonviolent resistance.

The attacker gradually loses divisive emotions in relation to the victim: fear, anger, hatred, indignation, pride, vanity, scorn, contempt, disdain, disgust, anxiety, worry, apprehension. These feelings are not merely thwarted or suppressed by the use of nonviolence; their very basis is uprooted.

The art of jiu-jitsu is based on a knowledge of balance and how to disturb it. In a struggle of moral jiu-jitsu, the retention of moral balance seems to depend upon the qualities of one's relationship to moral truth. Hence part of the superior power of the nonviolent resister seems to lie in the nature of his character.

He must have primarily that disposition best known as love—an interest in people so deep, and determined, and lasting as to be creative; a profound knowledge of or faith in the ultimate possibilities of human nature; a courage based upon a conscious or subconscious realization of the underlying unity of all life and eternal values or eternal life of the human spirit; a strong and deep desire for and love of truth; and a humility that is not cringing or self-deprecatory or timid but is rather a true sense of proportion in regard to people, things, qualities and ultimate values. These human traits of love, faith, courage, honesty and humility exist in greater or less strength in *every* person. By self-training and discipline they can be developed sufficiently to make a good nonviolent "soldier" out of any ordinary human being. Of course, leaders of a nonviolent movement require these qualities to an unusual degree, just as generals require military qualities more highly developed than those of the common soldier.

Love is the most important of all these qualities of the nonviolent person; it may even be considered the origin of all the others. If the word "love" in such a context seems too sentimental, call it a sort of intelligence or knowledge. This love must be strong and clear-sighted, not mawkish or sentimental. It does not hint that it is going to "do good to" the other person, nor does it make a parade of itself. It must be patient and full of insight, understanding and imagination. It must be enduring, kind and unselfish. It is wonderful but it is not superhuman or exceedingly rare. We have all seen such love in many mothers of all classes, nations and races, as well as in the best teachers. Its creativeness in these instances is well known.

If through love for your enemy you can create in him respect or admiration for you, this provides the best possible means by which your new idea or suggestion to him will become an auto-suggestion within him, and it will also help nourish that auto-suggestion.

Anger, as well as love, can be creative, for both are expressions or modes of energy. But love contains more energy and endurance than anger. Love involves the very principle and essence of continuity of life itself. If considered as an instrument, it can be more efficiently and effectively wielded, has better aim, has a better fulcrum or point of vantage, than anger. Love gains a stronger and more lasting approval from the rest of mankind. The probabilities in favor of its winning over anger in the long run are strong.

But if one party to a contest cannot develop toward the conflict or toward his opponent an attitude that is creative or akin to love, he should certainly be honest and true to himself. "Unless I am, in fact, so much of a seer to be a lover of my enemy," says Hocking, "it is both futile and false to assume the behavior of love; we can generally rely on the enemy to give such conduct its true name."[13] As long as men have uncontrollable anger or enmity in their feelings it is better to express it honestly and courageously than to be hypocritical and refuse to fight out of cowardice. In reference to such a situation Gandhi once said to me, "If you have a sword in your bosom, take it out and use it like a man." Christ, searching for a change in men more profound and important than immediate external acts, told them to get rid of anger and greed, knowing, I believe, that if this took place, war would disappear.

Courageous violence, to try to prevent or stop a wrong, is better than cowardly acquiescence. Cowardice is more harmful morally than violence. The inner attitude is more important than the outer act, though it is vitally important always to be true to oneself, to make one's outer conduct a true reflection and expression of one's inner state. Fear develops out of an assumption of relative weakness. Since all men have the innate possibility of moral strength, to be afraid is really a denial of one's moral potential powers and is therefore very harmful. Violence and anger at least show faith in one's own moral powers and thus provide at least a basis for further growth. He who refrains from fighting because he is afraid, really hates his opponent in his heart and wishes that circumstances would change so that he could hurt or destroy his opponent. The energy of his hate is present but suppressed. If one lacks the discipline or conviction to resist wrong or violence without counter-violence, then I agree with Gandhi that it is better to be violent than to be cowardly.[14]

But he who has the courage to fight and yet refrains, is the true nonviolent resister. Because the coward fears, he cannot love, and thus cannot be successful in nonviolent resistance. He cannot use this moral jiu-jitsu effectively. It is better to refrain from outward violent acts through fearless self-control of anger than to act violently, but getting rid of anger is the only sure way. True nonviolent resistance, where the outer act is an expression of inner attitude, gradually creates among all beholders an awareness of essential human unity. But if one's inner condition is of anger or hate, it causes a cowardly inconsistency with the superficial nonviolence of one's deed, which is soon detected by others and perhaps openly called hypocrisy. This inconsistency makes impossible any considerable increase in the awareness of essential unity.

As to the outcome of a struggle waged by nonviolence, we must understand one point thoroughly. The aim of the nonviolent resister is not to injure, or to crush and humiliate his opponent, or to "break his will," as in a violent fight. The aim is to convert the opponent, to change his understanding and his sense of values so that he will join wholeheartedly with the resister in seeking a settlement truly amicable and truly satisfying to both sides. The nonviolent resister seeks a solution under which both parties can have complete self-respect and mutual respect, a settlement that will implement the new desires and full energies of both parties. The nonviolent resister seeks to help the violent attacker to re-establish his moral balance on a level higher and more secure than that from which he first launched his violent attack. The function of the nonviolent type of resistance is not to harm the opponent nor impose a solution against his will, but to help both parties into a more secure, creative, happy, and truthful relationship.

3

WHAT HAPPENS

WHAT MORE IS THERE about the subtle interplay of forces operating during the struggle? For purposes of explanation, we may somewhat arbitrarily analyze and consider these forces in two groups: those which are mainly unconscious and those which are mainly conscious. In operation they are all inextricably mingled, but we can understand the matter better by discussing these processes as if they were separate.

One of these processes is what psychologists call suggestion. The conduct of the nonviolent resister suddenly presents the violent assailant with these startling new ideas: that the dispute can be settled calmly and amicably; that calm conduct is more dignified, more decent, more efficient, more worthy of respect than violence; that there may be something in the world more powerful and desirable than physical force; that the position of the attacker is much less favorable than he at first thought; that perhaps the two parties are not really enemies after all.

The attacker, at this moment, is in a most receptive and suggestible state, as we pointed out in the previous chapter. He is excited and, because of his wonder at the new ideas evoked by his nonviolent opponent, his attention is spontaneously concentrated on these new ideas. Under such conditions the process of suggestion acts most potently.

It is well known that suggestion, which is "essentially a process of the unconscious,"[1] is both powerful and lasting. The spectacle of bravely endured suffering along with all the surprises and uncertainty of the situation, creates emotion in the attacker. If there is a crowd present, it tends to heighten his suggestibility. These suggestions tend to change his inner attitude.

Or we may state it thus. If you want to conquer another man, do it not by outside resistance but by creating inside his own personality a strong new impulse that is incompatible with his previous tendency. Reinforce your suggestion by making it an auto-suggestion in him, so that it lives by his energy instead of by yours. And yet that new impulse is not to conflict directly with his former urge, but to divert and blend with it and absorb it, so as to use the full psychological energy of both impulses. That is the wisest psychological dynamics and moral strategy.

The new ideas in the astonishing situation tend strongly to stimulate the attacker's imagination. The Nancy school of psychology maintains that imagination and suggestion together are much stronger than conscious will power, so that if a person consciously wills and thinks that he desires to accomplish a given purpose, while his imagination is filled with ideas of his inability to accomplish it or of some contrary desire, then he will surely fail in the task. Baudouin states it as the "law of reversed effort." He says, "When the will and imagination are at war, the imagination *invariably* gains the day."[2]

If this be so, it may be that the ideas thus suggested to the attacker gradually capture his imagination and conquer his will to defeat the victim by violence. The Freudians show how much more powerful is a repressed wish than an opposing conscious desire. Possibly a suggestion acting imaginatively in the subconscious is as powerful as a repressed wish.

The sight of a person voluntarily undergoing suffering for a belief or an ideal moves the assailant and beholders alike and tends to change their hearts and make them feel a kinship with the sufferer. There are two reasons for this. First, our ancestors from the dawn of life have suffered pain and deprivation so extensively and intensely in the long course of evolution that suffering is very familiar to our entire nervous system. Indeed, it is almost habitual to the human species. Probably the nervous system is more responsive to stimuli associated with pain than to any other type of stimulus. Hence the sight of suffering causes an involuntary sympathetic response in the nervous system of the beholder, especially in the autonomic nervous system. The response may be inhibited or crusted over by custom, prejudice or hostile emotions, but it is there, nevertheless, at least in the subconscious. Therefore, the spectacle of a nonviolent resister submitting voluntarily to bodily suffering for the sake of his cause rouses feelings of sympathy in the onlooker. If the sight is prolonged or frequently repeated, the effect is all the stronger. There seems to be a social as well as an individual subconscious, through which such feelings would function.[3]

A related process affecting the attacker is unconscious imitation. Imitation is a basic means of communication by which we learn to talk and walk, learn skilled manual trades, pick up gestures and postures of our elders, follow our leaders—a limitless range of conduct. It lasts throughout life. Rivers tells us that "unwitting imitation is the most effective."[4]

When an attacker watches his victim's actions and comes to respect his courage, be it ever so little, he begins unconsciously to imitate him and thus his anger tends to subside. The James-Lange theory of the emotions adds weight to this conjecture. For reasons already considered, the peaceful contestant is less likely to be influenced toward violence by suggestion and imitation.

"War," according to Clausewitz, the great military strategist, "is a constant case of reciprocal action, the effects of which are mutual."[8] Again, Lieut-General von Caemmerer, in his *Development of Strategical Science,* says, "Every action in war is saturated with mental forces and effects. . . . War is a constant reciprocal effect of action of both parties."[9] This is true also of a conflict between individuals.

This factor of imitation also helps explain the futility of violence as a means of solving conflicts.

Suppose A attacks B, and B responds with violence. While part of B's response is purely instinctive and defensive, part of it also is unconscious imitation of A. So anger, resentment, hatred and revenge, in the process of reciprocal imitative violence, mount higher and enter more tensely into the personalities of the combatants, consuming all their energies, to the point of utter exhaustion or destruction.

Nonviolent resistance is a means of communicating feelings and ideas. It uses facial expressions, bodily gestures and the tone of voice, just as in all personal communication. In prolonged situations it may also use writing and printing. Its means of expression are as ample as those of any language. Even in situations where words can be used little or not at all, conduct, as indicated above, itself may be a rapid, accurate, and efficient means of communication.[10]

Nevertheless, the ideas to be conveyed are so unusual that the understanding of them by the recipient may be slow or incomplete. At first and perhaps for some time, the understanding will be more emotional than intellectual. Therefore, the success of the communication does not depend upon the extent of formal or book education of either party to the conflict. The idea itself is no more complex than that of war, for both involve discipline and control. In waging war, fear must be controlled, while anger is deliberately intensified and directed against the enemy; in nonviolent resistance, both anger and fear are controlled. Both anger and fear are elemental and similar emotions, and one control is no more complex than the other, nor are the ideas to be conveyed in either case.

There is both an emotional and an intellectual element to be transmitted—both feelings and ideas. There will be difficulties arising from the unusualness of the feelings and ideas, but no more difficulties arising from inadequacy of means than in the case of any other sort of language.[11]

Another largely unconscious process at work is the creative power of trust and expectation evinced by the nonviolent resister. He tries to give concrete and repeated evidence of his trust in the decency and reasonableness of the violent attacker, and of his expectation that this fine spirit, perhaps only latent at the start, will grow stronger until it informs, controls, and changes the assailant into nonviolent and kindly ways. This belief gives the resister hope, and he acts and holds himself in an attitude of expectancy and trust. Trust is subtly but powerfully creative. An example of this was shown by Gandhi in going to the second Round Table Conference at London in 1931. Although no results of it were then visible in the British government, there is evidence of considerable effect upon numerous persons who met Gandhi privately at that time.[12]

Psychologists tell us that the greater part of our mind is subconscious, beneath the surface, just as the preponderant bulk of an iceberg exists unseen below the water level. Forces that operate upon a person's subconscious, whether of suggestion, imagination-stimulus, imitation, communication or trust, have a greater effect than forces that operate only or chiefly upon the conscious mind and conscious feelings. This presumably holds true of a group as well as of an individual.

The analogy may be carried further. When an iceberg drifts into warm waters the submerged part gradually melts, showing little change above the water level. But after the melting underneath has gone far enough, sometimes the entire iceberg suddenly turns over and thereafter looks entirely different. Such sudden reversals can also occur in people as a result of forces acting a long time on the subconscious. It is not a miracle, but merely an instance of the operation of forces which we usually ignore. The analogy would tend to explain in part some of the impressive results of Gandhi's march to the sea in 1930, to make salt in defiance of the British government.

The total effect of these psychological processes taking place in the mind and heart of the violent opponent can best be described by the word "conversion." Probably the process is analogous to that of religious conversion, though in this case the change is moral rather than religious. The process may be explained as follows:

Every civilized person possesses in either his conscious or subconscious mind a store of elementary moral memories. Some of these are myths, fables, stories or other fictitious events which, as a child, he took for realities; some are moral relationships or moral standards impressed upon the individual at various stages in his development. Some of these have been repressed because they were inconsistent with subsequent courses of conduct. Others have been forgotten simply from lack of use or lack of attention. Each such residue of former beliefs or impressions is composed of representational, emotional and motor factors associated into a unit, and each of these units seems to have more or less psychic energy.

During a prolonged struggle between a nonviolent resister and his opponent, the psychological processes which we have described, together with the emotional and moral perturbation caused thereby, apparently recall to consciousness some of the forgotten elemental fragments of moral memories, dissociate some of the complexes that have been controlling the opponent's conduct, transfer their emotional tone and psychic energy to some of the revived memories and form new combinations.

Along with this shifting of the representational, feeling and motor factors of the psychic units, and their reassociation into new "constellations," the experiences of the struggle also tend to induce in the attacker a sublimation of his desires and energies, lifting them to a more social level, redirecting them in a more inclusive synthesis in which they can be reconciled with the ideals of human association.[13]

Nonviolent resistance in complete form is a dramatization of the idea of essential human unity. Therefore, with all the subtle power of genuine drama, it works upon the mind and heart of the opponent. In this drama the movement and confronting of ideas and forces causes in both the opponent and the spectator a clearer and profounder realization of human relations, a reconciliation of impulses and an illumination, enlargement and enrichment of consciousness. It brings about a more highly organized and more delicately balanced synthesis of the elements in the spectator's experience, an inner organization "less wasteful of human possibilities"[14] than that which prevailed in him before. It reveals the power of the human spirit to triumph over suffering and apparent disaster.

The psychological nature of nonviolent resistance may well be considered a form of what Rivers calls "manipulative activity." In discussing different modes of reaction to danger, he says:

"In the presence of danger, man, in the vast majority of cases, neither flees nor adopts an attitude of aggression, but responds by the special kind of activity, often of a highly complex kind, whereby the danger may be avoided or overcome. From most of the dangers to which mankind is exposed in the complex conditions of our own society, the means to escape lie in complex activities of a manipulative kind which seem to justify the term I have chosen. The hunter has to discharge his weapon, perhaps combined with movements which put him into a favourable situation for such an action. The driver of a car and the pilot of an aeroplane in danger of collision have to perform complex movements by which the danger is avoided."[15]

We may say that nonviolent resistance is a sort of moral manipulative activity in which the factors used and operated upon are largely psychological.

It may clarify our thinking somewhat to remember that we are not considering two static entities, an angry person versus a kindly person. We are dealing with two natures and an environment, each of which is mobile and changing, constantly acting on the other, influencing, changing, then responding to the new condition thus created.[16]

Another process develops after the struggle has proceeded for some time, namely, that of reassuring the violent party. Much of the latter's original basis of anger or fear is removed. He finds that the resister does not bear enmity toward him, that at least his "better self" and potentialities are respected instead of humiliated. He finds his original desires so illuminated and transmuted that in their new form they may be more easily satisfied. He finds the resister always ready to negotiate, always showing and inviting him to take a dignified way by which he, the assailant, may quickly regain his self-respect and public esteem. Since he has been provided with a satisfactory road for action, he is not left with what Graham Wallas called a "balked disposition."

Then comes the stage of what is known as "integration." In a very thoughtful book, *Creative Experience,* M. P. Follett shows that either voluntary submission of one side, struggle and victory of one side over the other, or a compromise, are all highly unsatisfactory and productive of further trouble. She then explains a fourth way, "integration."[17]

Integration is arrived at by first analyzing the expressed desires of the opponents into their underlying, fundamental meanings. To take a simple case, an insistence on having a table in a certain place in a room might really mean a wish to have light on one's writing while working at the table, together with an inability to see how it could be secured in any other way. An individual's insistence upon following a given trade may mean a need for employment, a desire for money, and a desire to satisfy pride. A nation's insistence upon political control of a certain territory may mean a need for food and industrial raw material, a desire to satisfy pride, and an inability to see how the satisfaction of these needs can be made wholly secure in any other way.

In each case, integration consists of working out a wholly new solution, perhaps involving very different activities, which satisfies all or most of the fundamental desires and needs of both parties in a situation, and utilizes freely and fully the energies of both without balking or suppression. The integration requires preliminary analysis, then the invention of a new solution which gives free scope to the energies of all parties concerned. Inevitably the solution is satisfying all around.

It takes much creative intelligence and ingenuity to find integrations, and not all differences can be integrated immediately. Temporary compromises can be made, however, pending further search and alterations due to passage of time, ending in an ultimate integration.[18]

In this connection it is well to remember the importance of love. Love for an opponent makes possible a sympathetic appreciation of the real meaning of his apparent needs, contentions, positions and desires, and implies a willingness to approach them open-mindedly, creating the right atmosphere for an integration of both one's own and the opponent's interests to a higher plane of action. Love also induces a frame of mind in the opponent which leads him to understand *your* needs, contentions, etc. And it shows the opponent that you are so appreciative of his side of the case that he can safely trust you.

The principle of integration indicates that, as a method, nonviolent resistance does not by itself necessarily settle all the conflict. It may be said to solve most of the emotional part—the fear, anger, pride, etc.—while the rest of the conflict may have to be solved by keen and perhaps prolonged intellectual exploration, with the new emotional attitude always at its elbow to help over the tight places.

All this ebb and flow of feeling and action and discussion may take place in different order from that described above. Its temper and intensity may vary according to the circumstances and character of the persons involved. It might take a considerable time to work through. Between sensitive persons the course of feelings and actions might be almost instantaneous. With a very proud or self-deceiving person, or a hardened soldier or policeman as attacker, the actual violence might be severe, repeated and lasting before the change of attitude or heart of the attacker would come about. Yet even among such attackers the surprise and wonder would often be so great as to cause a far quicker about-face and solution than might at first be expected.

When a solution is found, there is satisfaction and good feeling, a finer attitude and action not only among the participants to the struggle but among all the onlookers and public. To have the finer potentialities of men flower forth and bear fruit enhances the morale of all who learn of it.

4

UTILIZING EMOTIONAL ENERGY

As a method of solving a conflict, nonviolent resistance is sounder than reciprocal violence, because it is more efficient.

The first reason for this is partly physiological. Anger, hatred, and fear make an enormous drain upon our energy.[1] Hatred eats up our energies and our imagination. If you hate a man sufficiently, you cannot get him out of your mind, you are attached to him, you are his slave. The thought of him is an obsession; it wastes most of your time.

In a violent struggle, these emotions persist after the combat itself ceases. A victory by violence means humiliation for the conquered. He has had to admit the winner's superiority for the moment, but he vows vengeance. His resentment seeks satisfaction as soon as possible. His original anger, repressed by circumstances, becomes hatred and longs for revenge and retaliation. He nurses his grudge. His sympathetic family or friends may make his case their own. Perhaps a feud or vendetta develops. There have been many instances of feuds lasting many generations. International enmities in Europe have lasted for centuries. Retaliation provokes counter-retaliation. The original evil or damage is vastly multiplied and absorbs an enormous amount of time and energy diverted from useful occupations.

This wider and slower-acting effect of revenge and resentment is usually overlooked or minimized by apologists for war and physical force. But it holds true whether the struggle is between two individuals, between one person and a group or between two or more groups, whether the groups be small or large. It holds true in varying degrees, whether the original combat ended with no permanent injury to either side, with some injury or with death. It runs through all forms—the spanking of a child, a fight, a criminal arrest and imprisonment, capital punishment, a lynching, a strike or riot, piracy, a military raid or "punitive expedition," a civil or international war. Rarely does a peace settlement bring full satisfaction, forgiveness and solution of the entire original conflict, so that both parties feel thoroughly happy and ready to go ahead without suspicion or resentment. Anger is thus inefficient in both methods and results.

The peaceful resister has to expand much energy, but he applies it more intelligently than does the violent man. He selects the really important forces in the environment and seeks to alter them.[2] The angry and violent man puts too much emphasis on immediate objects and too little on the ultimate impelling forces behind them. If he considers impelling forces, he does not analyze them sufficiently or go far enough back. He has to waste much energy because, as it were, he uses too short leverages in attempting to move or divert opposing objects or forces. The nonviolent resister, by using longer psychological leverages, may have to move more slowly sometimes, but the work is more efficiently done and tends to be more permanent.

What William Alanson White said of conflicting tendencies in the individual may be applied as well to a conflict between two persons:

> "The symbolization of the conflict, either in the dream or in the symptoms of the neurosis or psychosis, will contain elements representative of both factors, and also . . . no solution of the conflict can come about except by the satisfaction of both these diametrically opposed tendencies. It follows, too, that no conflict can be solved at the level of the conflict. That is, two mutually opposed tendencies can never unite their forces except at a higher level, in an all inclusive synthesis which lifts the whole situation to a level above that upon which the conflict rose."[3]

Violent struggle is an attempt to solve a contest "at the level of the conflict." The defeat of either party results in suppression or repression of the energy of the wishes or will of the defeated party, and this is certain to result in waste, friction and trouble sooner or later. The repressed energy of the thwarted or defeated person will eventually find an outlet, a sort of revenge. Nonviolent resistance, followed up with moderate wisdom, offers a solution which gives satisfactory scope for the energies of both parties. Often it enhances their energies, as a result of the subsequent good feeling. New associations open up new channels for pleasurable and fruitful activity. The synthesis of both energies is similar to what the Freudians call "sublimation."

The nonviolent resister does not want passive compliance from the attacker, such as would be temporarily secured by using successful counter-violence against him. He wants the full energy of the attacker's active help. Therefore he tries to make it easy and reasonable for the attacker to join forces in the new program. He knows that the pattern of a peaceful stimulus to the violent one is more harmonious, more "voluminous," and therefore more potent and efficient than a violent, *i.e.*, intense and painful, stimulus would be.

Peace imposed by violence is not psychological peace but a suppressed conflict. It is unstable, for it contains the seeds of its own destruction. The outer condition is not a true reflection of the inner condition. But in peace secured by true nonviolent resistance there is no longer any inner conflict; a new channel is found, in which both the formerly conflicting energies are at work in the same direction and in harmony. Here the outer condition truly reflects the inner condition. This is perhaps one reason why Gandhi called this mode of solving conflict *Satyagraha*—"holding to truth." Such a peace endures.

Whatever can overcome anger and fear must be in principle the opposite of them and stronger than they are. Usually we think of courage as the opposite of fear. But really courage is only a partial antithesis. Courage usually implies a readiness to fight, to risk oneself, to match strength against strength, intelligence against intelligence. Courage, like anger, implies an attempt to end the threat of the opposing force or person by driving it away, making it submissive or destroying it, but does not usually imply rising above it and utilizing its energy in a higher synthesis. That is to say, courage implies willingness to engage in conflict on the same plane in which the threatening force is found, perhaps because of an estimation of superior strength or perhaps because of a consciousness of or faith in a higher security, and this means trying to suppress the energy of the force opposed.

In contrast to courage, love involves not only a willingness to take risks and face the threatening force, but also a desire and usually an ability to lift the conflict to a higher plane, where it can utilize the energy of the opposing force in a higher integration or sublimation.

Love is stronger than fear and anger. It is stronger because it is able to manipulate and guide their energy. It is more intelligent and far-seeing. It is also stronger because it is a more inclusive sentiment than fear or anger or hate. Love means using in the moral sphere the principle of the resolution of forces, known to every schoolboy who has studied physics, instead of the wasteful principle of direct opposition and consequent waste of energy, which produces unsatisfactory and only temporary results. Love does something better than conquer, for conquest implies destruction, submission and suppression. Love is more intelligent and tries not to allow any energy to go to waste.

In so far as life is made up of a flow of energy, any principle is sound which increases the flow of energy, and makes possible the joining and mutual reinforcement of two or more channels of energy. An increase of life energy gives power and joy.

So love is a great principle in moral dynamics. It does not suppress or thwart the energy behind fear and anger but uses it, and finds ways to steer it into channels desirable to both parties to the conflict. Fear and anger both involve an idea of separation, a flight, a driving away or extinction. Love, on the other hand, involves the idea of unity and attraction. It is, therefore, the true opposite, the sound principle by which to eliminate fear, anger, pride, and all other divisive emotions and attitudes.

Problems of conflict cannot, however, always be solved by firm refusals, kindly spirit, a desire for settlement and prolonged thinking and discussion. Further action is often necessary for psychological completeness and in order to expand and exemplify ideas sufficiently to make a real settlement. William James pointed out that it is psychologically unhealthy to feel an emotion or impulse and not give it fairly prompt expression in action.[4] In certain situations and with certain people action must be immediate—action which makes for a new order and thereby resists the old order. We tend to believe that thought clarifies and should precede action as the architect's plan precedes the construction of a building, but in actual life action often precedes and clarifies thought and even creates it. A sudden uprush of creative energy from the subconscious may discharge immediately into action without becoming conscious thought or taking time to find words until later. Action may indeed be considered a mode of thought. Such action, if it is consistent with the principles of nonviolence, is not an expression of suppressed anger or indignation, but an immediate creative urge of the whole personality. In certain situations, such action is tremendously energetic and swift—a sudden surge of power that is almost explosive. It may clear the air like a flash of lightning and prove wonderfully refreshing. It may help to create new values.

Examples of this sudden and immensely energetic action are found in the Indian Nationalist movement of 1930. The widespread manufacture of salt in opposition to the government salt monopoly, the refusal to pay taxes, the picketing of liquor and opium shops, the combination of making homespun cloth and picketing shops selling foreign cloth are specific instances. These activities were nonviolent. They aimed at replacing a pre-existing order by a new order. They were intended to put an end, among the masses, to the pre-existing fear of the government, and to stimulate courage, self-reliance, self-respect and political unity. They actually had that effect in large measure.

Action of this sort often seems necessary in the case of young persons, young mass movements and young nations. The earlier stages of life are primarily motor in character, and at that period strenuous action must follow promptly after thoughts and feelings and may often precede thought and accompany feeling from its beginning. Perhaps certain pathological conditions of human relationships require sudden and drastic action to create a better order. There is evidence indicating that by 1930 the politico-economic relations between Britain and India had reached a state which was morally pathological.[5]

When we come to consider the evolution of the instinct of pugnacity, we find further assurance of the validity of the method of nonviolent resistance. Hocking, in his *Human Nature and Its Remaking,* already cited, has an exceedingly interesting discussion of this point,[6] which may be summarized as follows:

In its crudest form, pugnacity requires the destruction of its object. But with the higher animals and man, destruction results in a partial defeat of one's total wish. The conqueror has enough interest in the survival of his opponent to want to see the latter's chagrin and acknowledgement of him as victor. The feeling "I want destruction" becomes "I want revenge." But revenge likes to nurse itself and persist, and thus the conqueror tends to prolong the vanquished's life so as to enjoy his discomfiture to the utmost. And the intensity of hatred in the victim of ruthless revenge becomes a danger. So revenge develops into punishment. Punishment tries to inflict pain, but without permanent injury. It discriminates between the *evil* of the opponent's will and the will itself, just as revenge distinguishes between the will and the life. Punishment tries to get rid of "an evil element in the will of another while retaining the integrity of, and the regard for that will as a whole." In doing so, however, it results in some degree of bitterness or hatred that interferes with the cure of the will. The next step is a sort of therapeutic improvement, a discovery of a better way to cure an evil or defective element in an opponent's will. Kindness and friendliness induce a desire in the opponent's own mind and heart to get rid of the defect or difficulty—a sort of auto-suggestion that is most efficient. Human progress through these stages of development has brought the shrewdest men to realize that the earlier and cruder expressions of pugnacity and anger "are not what the human being, on the whole, wants." What a person really wants is the richest and fullest possible expression of his energy. To attain this completely, there must be an equally rich and full expression of energy by all other persons.

"The doctrine of pacifism," says Trotter, "is a perfectly natural development, and ultimately inevitable in an animal having an unlimited appetite for experience and an indestructible inheritance of social instinct."[7] Altruism is, he observes, "a characteristic of the gregarious animal, and a perfectly normal and necessary development in him of his instinctive inheritance. The biologist . . . is aware that altruism . . . is the direct outcome of instinct, and that it is a source of strength because it is a source of union."[8]

Perhaps the East, as expressed by Buddha, Hindu ethics, the Jainas, Lao-tzü, Jesus and Gandhi, has studied human behavior more profoundly than any modern Westerners have yet succeeded in doing. The Oriental terminology may be different from ours but that does not make the conclusions less wise. The dense population and prolonged ages of intense social experience of India, China and other Asian civilizations brought about an insight and realization of the psychological validity of nonviolent resistance. Modern development of swift means of communication and transportation, the shocks and suffering of modern war and totalitarianism and the researches of Western psychology are perhaps tending to have the same effect as the dense population and long-sustained experience of the East, thus, maybe, preparing the Western mind to realize the same truth.

5

HOW IS MASS NONVIOLENCE POSSIBLE?

THE WISDOM OF THE EAST is gradually being approached in the West by way of scientific psychology and analysis. Many of our social problems will reach solution only after we apprehend more clearly the processes of our own thinking and emotions. A full understanding of conflict, between groups as well as between individuals, requires comprehension of the dynamic aspects of fear and anger, and of their results in action.

Fear and anger are closely allied. They have the same origin or purpose: to separate a person from a living creature, force or situation considered by the person to be painful, threatening or dangerous to his comfort or well-being, the easy action of his instincts or his very existence. If the person feels that he is stronger than the threatening force or situation, the emotion is anger, while if he estimates the danger as stronger than himself (including his skill), the emotion is fear.[1]

"In anger the removal may be effected by driving it (the threatening object) from the environment, destroying its consistency, or, if it is a threatening posture in another animal the removal may consist of merely changing the aggressive posture of the opponent into a submissive one."[2]

Hate is a sort of deferred or thwarted anger. The hated person or force is too strong to be removed or destroyed, and yet not strong enough to cause flight or abject submission. Therefore the person puts up with it, wishing all the time to destroy or harm it but not quite daring to do so, waiting for an opportunity to weaken or destroy it, but restraining his anger from blazing forth into open combat.

It seems from this that fear is always a sense of impending or possible loss of something considered valuable. The basis of both fear and anger is thus the same. If the threat of loss is wholly removed, the fear and anger also disappear.[3]

The instinct of flight corresponds to or operates along with the emotion of fear, while the instinct of pugnacity corresponds to or accompanies the emotion of anger. These instincts have the same purpose as these emotions—to separate oneself from a painful or threatening force or situation.

This common motive or basis of these pairs of emotions and instincts—flight: fear; pugnacity: anger—explains how mass nonviolent resistance is possible and also practical. We know that the elemental instinct of flight and its corresponding emotion, fear, can be controlled and disciplined by military training. Ages of war have taught us that this control and discipline are practical and effective. Since that is possible, it is equally possible to control and discipline the parallel and equally elemental instinct of pugnacity and emotion of anger.

It may be said that the discipline of emotion and instinct involved in war is feasible because courage comes to its aid. Courage seems to grow out of either a perception of superior strength, skill, endurance or security, or the superiority of the instinct for preservation of the human race over that of individual self-preservation, as where a mother sacrifices herself for her offspring.

But it is conceivable that in the case of nonviolent resistance there is another sort of courage, growing out of a different type of strength, skill, endurance or security; or perhaps here, too, there may be a more far-seeing factor operating for the preservation of the human race. Mankind has had more experience with the discipline of war than with the discipline of nonviolent resistance, but that does not make the creation and maintenance of the latter discipline intrinsically more difficult, once the matter is fully understood. The new discipline probably is quantitatively more difficult, because it involves control of both fear and anger, but it is not qualitatively or intrinsically more difficult, because both these emotions are similar in origin and in ultimate purpose, namely, human-preservation through individual self-preservation.

The human race has perhaps developed enough knowledge and intelligence for a larger number of its leaders to begin to grasp the possibilities of this novel discipline.

The possibility of altering the expression of pugnacity and creating this new discipline will be readily appreciated by students of psychology who are acquainted with Pavlov's researches on conditioned reflexes. Without attempting here to explain the conditioned reflex, it may be stated that Pavlov was able again and again, at will, to alter a dog's response to a destructive or painful stimulus from one of anger or defense to one of assimilation. A dog's digestive reflex may be made to stop appearing in the presence of food, and instead to appear upon feeling pain from an electric shock or a burn of an acid on the skin. The reflex may be reconditioned to a new stimulus which was just the opposite sort from what would be expected.

John B. Watson's experiments showing that a newborn baby has only two fears, that of falling and of a sudden loud noise, suggest that all other and more complex fears are conditioned reflexes.[4] This would tend to support the idea of war as being in part a mass-conditioned reflex. To the extent that it is such, that part of it may be altered and re-conditioned, just as much as any other. Or if friendly behavior or kindness can be considered in part a conditioned reflex, we may recondition that part of it to respond to hostile treatment. Of course both war and nonviolent resistance are much more than reflexes or instinctive actions, for they involve complex sentiments and conscious discipline. Nevertheless, the instinctive or reflex elements in war are capable of further alteration and discipline.

But is not human nature too weak for this new discipline? Doesn't this discipline make too heavy a drain on the resources of idealism, sentiment, emotion and moral character of ordinary mankind? It is said to take four years to make a good private soldier. New habits take time to become firm. This is as true of the control or discipline of anger as it is of the discipline of fear. One cogent example of what ordinary people can do when well-trained in nonviolence is the successful campaign of the peasants of Bardoli, India, described in Chapter One.

Napoleon once said that the value of discipline is seventy-five per cent of all the elements that go to make success in battle. Marshall Foch wrote, "Discipline constitutes the main strength of armies."[5] The Duke of Wellington observed that "habit is ten times nature."[6] This is just as true of the nonviolent discipline as of the discipline of violence. Gandhi realized this when he called off the struggle for

Indian political independence in 1922 after the Chauri-Chaura riots. He was sure that nonviolent resistance was the only way by which India could gain her political freedom. He tried to teach and train India to use that weapon. But when many did not understand the new method or failed in their self-control so that there were riots in Bombay in November 1921 and again in Chauri-Chaura in early 1922, he saw that they were not sufficiently disciplined. He could no more wage his kind of war with followers so undisciplined than Napoleon or Foch could win *their* kind without discipline. Therefore he declined battle. That did not mean that the *method* was a failure, but only that the new discipline was not sufficiently understood nor the training sufficiently prolonged. His hostile Indian critics in this matter did not understand the new method. Some of his formal opponents understood him better and appraised the power of his weapon more truly. One of these was Sir George Lloyd, who reportedly told Drew Pearson in 1929: "You can't go on arresting people forever . . . not when there are 319 million of them. And if they had taken [Gandhi's] next step and refused to pay taxes! God knows where we would have been."[7]

The failure at that time through lack of discipline no more proves that nonviolent resistance is ineffective, futile or impossible than the many routs and flights in battle prove that armies and violence are ineffective and absurd. Nor do the deaths and sufferings of nonviolent resisters in the past prove any more in this respect than the deaths and wounds of war. This was the first attempt to organize and discipline a large army of nonviolent resisters. Is it surprising that there was enough indiscipline and misunderstanding to make it necessary to call a halt, execute a strategic retreat, and begin to reform the ranks and train them more intensively and fundamentally?

As a matter of fact, there was proportionately more misunderstanding and lack of discipline among the literate and "intelligentsia" of India than among the illiterate peasantry. This is natural, because absorption of Western ways of thinking was an influence in favor of Western ways. Mental habit is strong, and so it was not easy for the intelligentsia to understand this new concept and discipline. This largely accounts also for the misunderstanding of Gandhi in the West. Up till now, pacifists have not sufficiently realized either the possibilities of joint, corporate action in nonviolent resistance, nor the necessity for discipline, nor the kind and intensity and many-sided details of that discipline.[8]

"Passive resistance," as Bertrand Russell pointed out during World War I, "if it were adopted deliberately by the will of the whole nation, with the same measure of courage and discipline which is now displayed, might achieve a far more perfect protection for what is good in national life than armies and navies can ever achieve, without demanding the carnage and waste and welter of brutality involved in modern war."[9]

It may be said, "You have named certain instances when non-violent resistance has been successful, but there have been countless exceptions, so many that the exceptions are the rule." I grant the death of Jesus and the Christian martyrs, the slaughter of innocent thousands by Jenghiz Khan and Tamerlane, the tortures of the Albigenses, the lynchings of Negroes and countless other instances. Some of these people, like many soldiers, won or established their causes even though they lost their own lives. Neither they nor their methods were any more "futile" than those of soldiers. But perhaps most of them did not show true nonviolent resistance.

The failures and apparent futilities of nonviolent resistance in the past have been due, very largely, to lack of discipline, as well as to lack of understanding of the full implications and requirements of the method. Of course there are sure to be some casualties and losses under it, even at its best. But provided there is discipline and leadership which fully understands the psychological mechanisms and the moral and spiritual elements involved, I am convinced that the losses will be much less than in violent war. The calculus of moral probabilities gives this answer, and historical examples of its intelligent practice prove it, as we have already seen. Even in the case of individual encounters, if nonviolence is used consistently, the chances of failure or death are less, I believe, than if violence is relied upon. Even where death occurs, the cause for which the man died may triumph in spite of his death or even because of it. The test of nonviolence is not only whether it can achieve success for its cause, but also whether it can achieve it with less destruction of life, physical injury or destruction of property than when violence is used. On both these points nonviolent resistance wins, provided the discipline, understanding and leadership are sound.

An army can be effective without every soldier in it, or even a majority of them, being individual paragons of intelligence and military virtue. Discipline removes most of the effect of their individual weaknesses and adds momentum to their virtues. It is the same with a group or army of disciplined nonviolent resisters. If their leaders have the requisite attitude, understanding and intelligence, the rank and file may, at the start, be ordinary human material. The new training and discipline will improve them enormously, as is also asserted for military discipline. Presumably, the smaller the group, the more complete the discipline and understanding must be. Lone individuals using nonviolent resistance require more self-control and ability than is needed for a disciplined group. But even here the inner attitude and emotional understanding and control are much more important than any intellectual ability or experience in the rough-and-tumble world. Indeed, in certain situations so-called "intellect" and experience count for almost nothing.

Hence it is not necessary that every single person in a nation seeking freedom by nonviolent resistance must be fully disciplined to nonviolence, any more than every single citizen in a nation at war must be fully disciplined for active battle and wholly fearless under attack. Yet it is possible for whole nations to *understand* the idea and to be so self-disciplined as to give the "troops" hearty support and do nothing (as by outbreaks of anger and violence, riots, etc.) to interfere with their operations, just as it is possible in the case of whole nations supporting their armies in time of war.

Violence is based upon fear and anger and uses them to the utmost. We have seen that these two emotions are based on the idea of separation, of division. Nonviolent resistance, on the other hand, is based upon the idea of unity. The hypothesis of nonviolent resisters is that the strongest factor in human beings, in the long run, is their unity—that they have more in common as a human family than as separate individuals. The basic assumption of these creative men of peace is that their opponents, no matter how externally forbidding, and no matter what their past history, are at bottom decent and have in their hearts at least a spark of good spirit which can eventually be aroused and strengthened into action. Nonviolent resisters have sound biological, psychological and historical evidence for this belief. If it were not true, the human race would long ago have ceased to exist.

6

THE WORKING OF MASS NONVIOLENT RESISTANCE

Assuming that the discipline of nonviolence can be and has been attained, how does it actually work in group or mass use?

Since war is the most highly developed and best understood mode of mass struggle, we will find our explanation first from authorities on the science and art of war.

Marshal Foch showed clearly by many examples that the method of war is primarily psychological, or what he calls "moral":

> "Proofs and instances could be given indefinitely of that great importance of morale in war. Von der Goltz himself tells us that: 'It is not so much a question of destroying the enemy troops as of destroying their courage. Victory is yours as soon as you convince your opponent that his cause is lost.' And again; 'One defeats the enemy not by individual and complete annihilation, but by destroying his hopes of victory.' "[1]

Marshal Saxe remarked: "The secret of victory lies in the hearts of human beings."[2] Napoleon stated that "in war, the moral is to the physical as three is to one."[3] Caemmerer, speaking of Clausewitz's book on war says, "As he pictures war, the struggle between the spiritual and moral forces on both sides is the center of all."[4] Captain B. H. Liddell Hart wrote that World War I confirmed "the immemorial lesson of history—that the true aim in war is the mind of the enemy command and government, not the bodies of their troops, that the balance between victory and defeat turns on mental impressions and only indirectly on physical blows."[5]

The object of nonviolent resistance is partly analogous to this object of war. War seeks to demoralize the opponent, to break his will, to destroy his confidence, enthusiasm and hope. Nonviolent resistance demoralizes the opponent only to re-establish in him a new morale that is finer because it is based on sounder values. Nonviolent resistance does not break the opponent's will but alters it; does not destroy his confidence, enthusiasm and hope but transfers them to a finer purpose.

As Hocking points out, "Morale is at the bottom a state of will or purpose."[6] It seems to rest largely upon such factors as the individual soldier's confidence in himself, in his comrades, in his army, in his leaders, in the methods used, in the cause for which the war is being waged, in his government, in the civilians of the nation behind them all. It also contains such elements as habit, tradition, humor, a sense of being merged into the larger unity of the army, appreciation of risk and a relish for adventure.[7]

Suppose a group of nonviolent resisters were opposed to a company of soldiers, and that the soldiers attempted clubbing tactics or bayonet work. Let us assume also that the civilians have been nonviolent from the start and there is no shooting by the soldiers. But suppose there is some violence by the soldiers, and arrests of the civilians. Conceivably a troop commander might lose his head and cause a massacre; such a case will be discussed later. Omitting this consideration for the present, let us further assume that the cause is so strong that as fast as any are arrested, others come to take their places. What, presumably, would be the effect of this on the morale of the soldiers?

To a certain extent, the effect would be the same as that described in the preceding chapter where an individual person violently attacks a nonviolent resister. But the discipline and habits of the soldiers would largely prevent this from happening at first. The individual soldier's will has become merged with the general will of the army, and wholly subordinated to that of the commanding officer. He is used to rough tactics and is not at all squeamish about inflicting pain and injury on others.

Nevertheless, as Rivers points out, "One of the chief results of military training is to increase the suggestibility of the private."[8] He notes this suggestibility chiefly in relation to the officers, but no doubt the soldiers are also suggestible in relation to the acts and conduct of their opponents or "enemies" because such acts and conduct are the whole object toward which the morale of the soldiers has been built up. This is also indicated by Clausewitz: "War is a constant state of reciprocal action, the effects of which are mutual." Caemmerer notes also that "every action in war is saturated with mental forces and effects. . . . War is a constant reciprocal effect of action of both parties."[9] This fact then would presently tend to offset the discipline and hardness of the soldiers.

The conduct of the nonviolent civilians would cause surprise in the individual soldier and thus start him thinking. Frederick the Great wrote, "If my soldiers began to think, not one would remain in the ranks." As soon as a soldier begins to think of certain sorts of things, he begins to be an individual, to separate himself from the mass mind, the will and personality of the army. If, then, the soldier is made to think for himself in the midst of a conflict, a start has been made toward the disintegration of his morale. I do not mean to say that modern soldiers do no thinking at all, but in these days of mass communications a very large proportion of all people do very little thinking for themselves. And among soldiers, this is still more true over a still wider range of affairs.

As the struggle proceeds, suppose the nonviolent civilians maintain their discipline and keep cheerful but also keep stating their side of the case earnestly and in all sincerity. Sooner or later the soldiers will begin talking about it among themselves. The total absence of retaliation or vindictiveness even in looks or tone of voice, on the part of the civilians, contrasts effectively with the harsh or stern commands of their officers. The situation will tell on the nerves of both officers and soldiers. This sort of thing is new to them. They do not know how to treat it. "These civilians seem wholly inoffensive and harmless and honest. What is their crime? Why were we soldiers called out for such a job? We are for war work, but this is peace." Thus they will question in their minds and perhaps among themselves. They will begin to fraternize with the civilians and learn more about the dispute in which they are engaged. It will no longer appear to be a clear-cut case of right vs. wrong, but the opponent's case will appear to have elements of reason.

If the officers forbid them to fraternize with the opponents, the soldiers may think that the order is stupid or that the officers are timid. This lessens respect for their officers and lowers morale.

If there really is solid truth in the position of the nonviolent resisters, the soldiers will presently begin to question the validity of
their own cause. They may become slack in obeying orders. They
will see no good to be gained by their being there, and no evil or
danger to be averted. "When doubt comes, morale crumbles."[10] The
Duke of Wellington put it forcefully: "No man with any scruples of
conscience is fit to be a soldier." One of the important elements in a
soldier's morale, as Hocking has indicated, is his consciousness of
being a protector.[11] If he is deprived of that, he feels useless and
perhaps a little absurd. There is no exhilaration in using violence
against nonviolent resisters. The soldiers may even feel that the authorities or their officers have morally let them down.

Meanwhile, the situation is unpleasant for the officers, too. If they
make any serious mistake, they may lose the respect of the private
soldiers as well as of the general public. If they order any shooting,
there is almost sure to be a wave of public indignation. They know
how to fight, but they feel that this situation is "a mess." As Lt.-Col.
Andrews says, "Officers naturally dread riot duty,"[12] and while there
is no rioting here, the situation is felt to be just as delicate, perhaps
even more so. Soldiers are trained for action but this encounter is
nearly all quiet. Inaction is notoriously hard on a soldier's morale.[13]

Someone may object that nonviolent resistance is so passive that it
would be fully as hard on the morale of those using it as on that
of the soldiers opposing them. Not so. The conduct of the nonviolent
resister is not one of mere passive waiting or endurance. Toward
his opponent he is not aggressive physically, but his mind and emotions are active. He wrestles constantly with the problem of per-
suading the latter that he is mistaken, seeking proposals for a better way out and examining his own cause and organization to see
what may be its mistakes or short-sightedness. He is thinking constantly of all possible ways of winning the truth for both sides. And
among his own group, he is ceaselessly active in strengthening the
organization, improving its members' unity, discipline and understanding, helping to remove every possible cause of reproach. He
is as busy as any top sergeant of a regiment.

The lives of most private soldiers are filled with monotony and
irresponsibility. The conduct of these civilians will be new to them
and will elicit their interest and attention.

The courage and persistence of the nonviolent resisters will call forth the admiration of the soldiers and onlookers or general public. All parties begin to feel that the authorities have chosen the wrong method. They tend to feel that this is a matter for a court or arbitration or discussion. This feeling makes rifts between the troops and the higher command or civilian authorities.

As the situation drags on, the officers become increasingly restive. It is undignified to have to proceed thus against harmless, decent, defenseless people. They begin to feel themselves in a ludicrous position. Neither the officers nor the enlisted men can feel that they are protecting anyone or any property, since it is evident that the nonviolent civilians pose no threat of harm.[14] That consciousness tends to lower self-respect. The near mutiny of British troops occupying the Ruhr after the World War I Armistice, while the "starvation blockade" of Germany was still in effect, affords a clear illustration. A more recent if less conclusive example is that of American soldiers who staged "demobilization strikes," in Germany and the Philippines in 1945.

Perhaps there has been a campaign to make the nonviolent resisters seem despicable. They have perhaps been accused of bodily uncleanliness, dirt, disorder, illiteracy, ignorance, bad manners, mental and moral degeneracy. They are said to be "beyond the pale," "barbarous," "beneath contempt," etc., etc. We all know this method of bolstering up one's own pride and self-esteem. It is easy to find faults in a stranger, or differences that seem like faults; and a little unconscious pharisaism helps immensely to increase one's morale and salve one's conscience. But the soldiers in immediate contact with the nonviolent resisters may find that in fact they are clean, orderly, well disciplined, determined, intelligent, "very decent" in behavior, and very courageous. It is impossible to be contemptuous of such men. And when respect begins, the instinct for fair play asserts itself. By that time, morale is not very prominent. That such things can happen even in unlikely circumstances is proved by the fraternizing between the German and Allied troops on the first Christmas of World War I. If at the beginning the nonviolent resisters are not very well disciplined, yet are faithful to their ideal, their discipline will grow.

Suppose one of the officers loses his head, or believes in "making an example" and teaching by terror, and orders the soldiers to fire on the unarmed nonviolent resisters, and many are wounded and killed. The effect is indeed electrical. The immediate beholders may be terror-stricken for a short time. But the news inevitably spreads, and the public indignation against the officer and soldiers will be overpowering. This was the case with the Jallianwala Bagh tragedy in India. By the manner of their death, the hundreds who died there did more to further the cause of Indian political freedom than could the deaths of three times that number in violent rioting or attack upon the army. News of the massacre was a blow to British prestige throughout the world, as well as to British self-respect.

There have undoubtedly been similar cases of violence by troops of every nation that likes to consider itself a "trustee" for other nations, tribes or races. A similar instance occurred in the United States in the winter of 1929, when Pennsylvania coal company police killed a miner on strike. Such deeds are not peculiar to any nation but only to a particular purpose and set of beliefs. The point to be emphasized is that nonviolent resistance, even in the extreme case where its users are killed, has a far higher probability of weakening the morale of the violent opponents and of promoting the aim sought for than violent resistance would have.

If the government uses police instead of soldiers, this process of morale destruction will operate somewhat differently. Police are usually drawn from the same district where they work, and so are not likely to be so prejudiced. They are more likely to be married men and so, through their wives, more open to public opinion. If many new police are brought in, their discipline will be weak and they will be apt to indulge in excesses which will rouse public opinion against the government as well as themselves.

What might happen where the soldiers use tear gas, or bomb attacks by airplanes? Nonviolence is not likely to incite such an act, but it has happened. In such an event there would temporarily cease to be direct effective contact between the soldiers and the nonviolent resisters. Therefore, the morale of the soldiers would probably not be weakened. The problem for the nonviolent resisters now becomes temporarily reduced to the endurance of physical suffering and caring for the wounded.

In war the sight of wounded men being sent back from the front lines, says Captain Liddell Hart, "tends to spread depression among the beholders, acting on morale like the drops of cold water which imperceptibly wear away the stone."[15]

This is not the case where nonviolent resisters are concerned. For a soldier, being wounded or suffering means the negation of the role for which he has been trained—to cause wounds and inflict suffering. For the nonviolent resister, however, it is only the extension to an extreme of his basic purpose: to touch people's feelings and make them think differently, and he is therefore prepared to meet it with loftier courage than the soldier can muster. For this reason, the sight of the nonviolent wounded creates a purer, wider, more active and more enduring sympathy and unity with their cause than does the sight of wounded soldiers. In nonviolent resistance the suffering is itself a weapon or means of winning. Hence, such casualties do not decrease the morale of the nonviolent resisters. Similarly, when nonviolent resisters are imprisoned they are not thereby rendered useless to their cause. Instead, their endurance of hardship increases the general sense of human unity and sympathy for their cause.

Sooner or later, there will be parleys between the nonviolent resisters' leaders and officers of the army or emissaries from the government. Such parleys mean contact, hence an opportunity further to convert the opponents, or, in military parlance, to alter their morale.

Whenever the violent opponents ask to negotiate, the leaders of the nonviolent party will enter into negotiations, even though it may seem that by refusing to do so and going on with the struggle the violent opponents may be compelled to yield, and even though the request may be or seem to be a stratagem on the part of the opponents to gain time or to break up the unity of the nonviolent party. This willingness to negotiate proves to the violent opponent and to the world that the nonviolent resisters are not seeking to humiliate their opponents, and thus paves the way for the conversion of the opponents and for the only kind of victory worth having. Some examples of this were Gandhi's negotiations with Viceroy Lord Irwin during the Indian struggle of 1930-31, and later with Viceroys Lord Linlithgow, Lord Wavell and Lord Mountbatten.

It should be remembered that ruthless deeds tend to become known to the world at large and then to lessen the respect of other nations for the nation indulging in them. The government in question, besides receiving foreign censure, will be severely criticized by its own more decent citizens. They may create a very considerable pressure of public opinion against the government and compel it to alter its tactics. It is true that distant civilians who have been blinded by their own pride and long-continued propaganda are very often harder to touch than the hostile soldier on the spot. The armchair warriors at home during Word War I were unbelievably cruel and hard, and worse in America than in England or France because they were farther away and felt realities less. Yet once their morale gets a little undermined, they crumble rapidly, for they lack the discipline of soldiers.

The experienced person will say that such events are always hidden by the censorship of such a government. Sometimes this is so. Acts of the American marines in Haiti and Nicaragua were hidden that way for months. The American government's treatment of the Japanese Nisei in concentration camps in World War II was practically ignored by the American press. The news of Jallianwala Bagh at Amritsar in India did not reach the United States for eight months after the event. But the tendency is for such news to leak out sooner or later. People of all nationalities go to all parts of the world nowadays. Travel and trade are ubiquitous. Newspaper reporters are always keen for scenting a "story," and as soon as they learn of a censorship anywhere they are still more eager. The modern press services have long stimulated people's curiosity. And if curiosity finds itself balked or thwarted, it will never rest till the story is known. And Western nations are all so jealous of one another that each is eager to learn and publish something discreditable to the others. (I am not trying to criticze, but merely to state facts,—weaknesses among those who are addicted to violence, against which the stronger forces of nonviolence will effectively operate.) Any considerable struggle in which one side rigidly sticks to nonviolent resistance with any degree of success makes wonderful news. It is so unusual and dramatic. Newspaper reporters and correspondents have a sense of "news value," and can be trusted to try hard to evade government censorship. The mere knowledge that censorship has been employed arouses doubt in neutral minds of the violent assailant's case. If, in the area where the struggle goes on, the opposing government does not permit the newspapers to publish adequate news of the struggle, the people cease to believe the official statements, and give credence instead to oral rumor or information passed about among themselves.

Of course powerful ruling groups and countries rely chiefly on pride, disdain and disgust to censor the news. They or their supporters vilify these protesting groups or nations, and the general repugnance thereby created acts as a screen against the truth. Many a trade unionist knows the truth of this out of his own hard experience. So also do the Negroes, Chinese and Indians, poor immigrants in the United States and many others.

But any oppressed groups anywhere, in non-Communist countries anyhow, may also be sure that sincere prolonged nonviolent resistance on their own part will surely break down barriers and rouse enough curiosity, respect and wonder, to reveal at least a part of the truth and thus effect a more satisfactory adjustment of the conflict. Whether all this applies in Communist lands I shall consider a few pages later.

In nonviolent resistance as practiced by Gandhi there is another element which serves to weaken censorship. That is his rigid adherence to truth. He never tolerated secrecy of any sort. He invited the police to meetings and answered all their questions fully. He always notified the authorities amply in advance of any action he planned to take which might affect them, and was frank about his beliefs and position. Examples of this may be found in his campaign in Champaran, his long letter to Viceroy Lord Irwin in March 1930, and his telegrams to Viceroy Lord Willingdon in December 1931 and January 1932. Such a policy gives the public full advance notice of what is likely to take place, and thus makes a subsequent censorship much more difficult to maintain. Clean fighting such as this retains every moral advantage of the noblest chivalry, *i.e.,* what General J. F. C. Fuller has called "the cultivation of respect in an enemy for or by his opponent"[16] Secrecy would indicate or seem to indicate fear as well as untruth, or suggest them with the effect of auto-suggestion, and thus would spoil the morale of the resisters and deprive the method of its power.

But the nonviolent resisters must realize that they cannot decrease the prestige of their opponents or create dissension among their opponent's supporters until they break through the censorship of governments, press associations, or popular disdain; that they cannot break through these censorships until they have conducted themselves with high excellence, discipline, unity, coherence, cleanness and courage so as to compel respect, admiration and wonder. Therefore, their chief efforts should be not in talking to reporters or appealing for help from outsiders, but with themselves, to increase their own discipline and organization, their courage, courtesy, intelligence, cleanness and order. They should strive for such details even as clean bodies, clean clothes, clean houses, clean streets, clean talk. These create self-respect and respect from others. Military discipline is thorough and detailed like this. Nonviolent discipline must be the same. Such resisters must realize that if ever they fail in their discipline and fall into violence, untruth, secrecy or disorder, they set back their cause and delay their victory; and if they do not recover their discipline, they will suffer complete defeat. For these reasons there is need for the utmost energy, determination, persistence and will-power on the part of nonviolent resisters, whether they be national groups or labor unions or what not. This discipline, chiefly directed toward themselves, will not arouse outside opposition. They will compel respect when they deserve it and not before. And when they can compel respect, they are on the road to upsetting their opponents' morale.

ONE MORE POLICY of ruthlessness must be considered, namely that of starvation. This was used against the Germans with fearful effect in World War I. But it is a weapon that cuts both ways. It not only weakened the Germans greatly during the war but so interfered with their recuperative ability after the "peace" that it reduced the prosperity of the whole world. The Allied bankers and merchants suffered from the loss of German purchasing power in the aftermath of World War I. Not only this, but the punitive approach of the Allies set the stage for Hitler's rise to power. Fortunately after World War II this policy, embraced in the Morgenthau Plan, was quickly abandoned in favor of democratization and Marshall aid.

Against smaller groups a government might attempt starvation, but if such groups are really in earnest, have a good cause, and maintain good discipline, their resistance will surely affect public opinion and lower the morale of their opponents. Compare, for instance, the effect of MacSwinney's hunger strike in prison during the Irish struggle for freedom.

Any persons who feel aggrieved by the policies of the ruling groups of either Great Britain or the United States may count on help from the strong desire of the peoples of those countries always to justify their conduct morally, to give it at least a moral tone or appearance.[17] When the Germans invaded Belgium in 1914, Britain and the Allies used this violation of treaty to stiffen their own morale and secure help from neutrals. It enabled them to play the part of chivalrous defenders of the weak. It served to cover up many mistakes, faults and evils of the Allies, and kept them all feeling splendidly self-righteous for several years, at least till the secret treaties leaked out. The political effect of this attitude of mind is a desire for and reliance upon prestige—a superiority complex which is designed to create an inferiority complex among other nations or races, and thus facilitate the task of dominating.

The maintenance of this prestige requires respect, awe or fear from others. Now if any of these Anglo-Saxon governments or ruling groups engage in harsh violence against a group of truly nonviolent resisters, the news surely leaks out sooner or later and lessens the prestige of that ruling group in the eyes of the rest of the world, as well as in the eyes of the more honest and intelligent persons in the nation in question. The highly moral attitude and tone of that government's professions begin to look thin and ludicrous. Its dignity and prestige are shaken and its morale weakened. Public opinion today all over the world condemns ruthless violence and cruelty as such, once the cloak of disgust, disdain or fear propaganda has been removed. Thus the need of those who rely on prestige for respect from the rest of the world, becomes a weak spot in their armor, the minute they do an act which does not deserve or actually win respect. The nonviolent resisters' weapon of love of truth is directed immediately at this weak spot and pushed home with all courage and fortitude.

It is true that the Germans under Hitler and the Communist Russians have persecuted, tortured, oppressed and destroyed human beings on a vaster scale than any known before in the history of the world. It might seem, then, that against such foes, organized mass nonviolent resistance would be futile folly, and that in view of man's weaknesses and examples of history, skepticism about the power of nonviolence against such people and such institutionalized ideas is only sensible. But if man had been wholly obsessed with the failures recorded in history, he would never have learned how to live in cities of over two million population, how to fly, to send messages by radio, or create a hydrogen bomb, to say nothing of many other things done for the first time in history. And though man is often weak, he can, by using the right means, become more often strong. Let the skeptic, therefore, suspend judgment until he has finished reading all this book and then has carried out some of the simple experiments suggested in the last chapter.

We can now see that nonviolent resistance "reduces the utility of armaments as instruments of policy," to use Madariaga's phrase.[18] It does so partly in direct and positive manner, proposing and aiding in the creation of new terms of settlement, new roads out of conflict. It also does so by disintegrating the morale of the opponent—the morale of troops, of commanders, of civil authorities and of their home civilian populations. The breakdown of the violent opponent's morale is really a change of heart. He does not merely become discouraged about fighting or about his power. He ceases to want in the same way the things he wanted before; he ceases to maintain his former attitude toward the resisters; he undergoes a sort of inner conversion. In the case of a very proud and obstinate opponent, there may have to be a complete outward defeat before the change of heart really takes place, but such a change is sure to come. In case of industrial strikes, nonviolent resistance would tend to raise doubts in the minds of the stockholders of the corporation involved. It tends to lower the prestige of any controlling power or group that is not acting as true servants of the people within their governance.

General (then Colonel) Fuller pointed this out as early as 1923:

"The principle of demoralization has for its object the destruction of this morale: first, in the moral attack against the spirit and nerves of the enemy's nation and government; secondly, against this nation's policy; thirdly, against the plan of its commander-in-chief; and fourthly, against the morale of the soldiers commanded by him. Hitherto, the fourth, the least important of these objectives, has been considered by the traditionally-minded soldier as the sole psychological objective of this great principle. In the last great war the result of this was—that the attack on the remaining three only slowly evolved during days of stress and because of a faulty appreciation of this principle during peace time."[19]

Nonviolent resistance operates to lower all these different kinds of morale, and it may be effectively aided by economic boycotts or in some extreme instances perhaps by non-payment of taxes.

We see, therefore, that nonviolent resistance is not wholly unlike the principles of military demoralization. It is merely a step further in the logic, and in military history.

Besides decreasing the opponent's morale, mass nonviolent resistance does much to enhance the morale and unity of those who use it. We have noted the unifying effect of the sight of voluntary suffering. This operates not only upon the resisters themselves but also, by sympathy, upon all beholders who hitherto may have been neutral. This happened repeatedly in India during the campaigns for national independence. The sincerity and earnestness of the sufferers, if the suffering continues long, convinces many others and wins them over to support the cause. The sight of leaders themselves enduring hardships, insults and wounds, going to jail, sacrificing their fortunes and lives for their cause is far more potent to produce increase of numbers, unity, enthusiasm, devotion and increase of effort than the sight, in violent war, of generals and politicians dwelling in comfort and safety and telling others what to do and how to fight. "The blood of the martyrs was the seed of the Church," and the same result comes in any situation where nonviolent methods are steadily used.

In situations where there is such rigid government censorship that little news of the oppression and violence of soldiers and police against the nonviolent resisters gets to the outside world, this unifying effect and winning of sympathy from neutral or timid onlookers is very important. The example of steady, long-continued nonviolent resistance creates within the censored area a public opinion that compels aid from all sorts of men who may have been entirely and strongly opposed to the resisters. Intellectual reasons for not joining the group crumble away, sometimes slowly, sometimes quickly. The feelings engendered by the prolonged sight of nonviolent suffering for a cause end differences of mind and also of feeling.

In situations that involve wide differences of custom or culture (*e.g.,* struggles for colonial independence or racial equality), it may take many months for the unifying effect of nonviolent resistance and its search for social truth to go far enough to bring success. Nevertheless, the process is sure and, if the method is faithfully adhered to, the result certain.

It may be that while the resisters are in jail, some of the conservative, selfish or comfort-loving members of their general group engage in "politics" and palaver with the opponents. This took place in India during the struggle for independence. As that sort of thing goes on, perhaps for months, the contrast between them and those who are suffering jail terms and hardships grows so glaring that more and more people turn away in disgust and mistrust from the politicians and pin their faith on those who are in jail. The politicians sense this loss of their prestige and are in turn compelled to follow the crowd and cease cooperating with the opponents.

This unifying power of nonviolent resistance may often take effect more rapidly than does the breaking down of the morale of the opponents. It is also a factor in that loss of morale. As time goes on, the access of numbers, strength and unity in the group of nonviolent resisters begins to impress the violent opponents, to fill them with misgivings, and thus to injure their morale still further. Strength compels respect, and in this case the respect is for moral qualities as well as for numbers or political power.

War also acts to unify nations engaged in it. But the unity engendered by nonviolent resistance is deeper, more closely knit and more permanent than that produced by war, for reasons already discussed. The unity of a nation at war is achieved at the expense of any higher unity, while the unity of the nonviolent group is not based on exclusion of the enemy.

If, as often happens,[20] the group or nation that is using nonviolent resistance has been under political, economic or social subjection for many years, it may have lost much self-confidence, self-reliance and self-respect. This new method of struggle tends to put an end to that weakness.

The contrast between the brutal deeds of the exasperated violent party and the nonviolent sufferings of the resisters is so startling as to produce in the ranks of the resisters a feeling of immense moral superiority. Presently the rage of the violent party leads them to make false statements or commit various stupidities which make the resisters realize that their superiority is intellectual as well as moral. This intellectual contrast grows still more marked if the resisters adhere faithfully to truth in all their words as well as actions. If the stimulus of these contrasts is continued long enough, the inferiority complex of the resisters' group vanishes and their self-respect, self-confidence and self-reliance steadily increase. Thus another element of their former disadvantage is done away with. Students of psychology have now learned what rulers have known for centuries—that an inferiority complex, firmly created in childhood and judiciously maintained by regular stimulus through the period of development, is the most potent of all methods of restraining independent creative action among individuals and masses of people. It makes them feel utterly helpless and deprives them of hope, imagination or will even to try to struggle, and in times of crisis it creates a fatal hesitation and lack of confidence. Hence this creative power of nonviolent resistance, putting an end to inferiority complexes, makes it a very important weapon for oppressed nations, classes and groups everywhere.

Another reason why mass nonviolent resistance is effective is that, like individual nonviolence, in course of time it wins for its users the support of public opinion. It is well known that the gaining of public opinion is one of the principal objects of war[21]

The techniques of "psychological warfare" played a very important part in World War II, and in large degree comprised the backbone of the Cold War of the 1940s and '50s. To use another term, it is recognized that the conflict is a "struggle for the minds of men."

Victories in war are imposing and terrifying, but the alliances and cooperation gained thereby are notoriously unstable. Such allies come more because it seems expedient than because they really want to. A victory by nonviolent resistance does not carry with it a further latent threat to harm anyone. It carries conviction of sincerity and friendship, whereas a victory through violence always has in it at least a suspicion of selfishness and possible further aggrandizement. In quality a victory by nonviolent resistance is far more gallant and joyous than one by violence can ever be. It requires no lying, distortion or suppression of the truth, no slaughter or threats. It leaves no bad conscience or bad taste in the mouth. The public opinion it gains is weighty and lasting.

Still another way in which mass nonviolent resistance operates is to end and clear away social defects, economic mistakes and political errors. The semi-military discipline of the resisters, the getting rid of bad habits, the learning to struggle without anger, the social unity developed, the emphasis on moral factors, the appeal to the finest spirit of the opponents and onlookers, the generosity and kindness required—all these constitute a social purification, a creation of truer values and actions among all concerned. If the struggle involves many people and lasts a long time, the discussion of the issues becomes so widespread, intense and detailed that much that was previously hidden or misunderstood is revealed and made clear to all. It is a period of great public education. The nature of the struggle and its prolongation bring into unmistakable action the real purpose of the two parties, and show a great many of the implications of their respective aims and attitudes not previously seen or understood. The struggle tests the sincerity of both parties. It corrects errors among the violent party, too. This evolution of more social truth is a gain to both sides. Like war, nonviolent resistance is a method of deciding great public questions, and this clearing away of errors is an essential part of the settlement of such great disputes. "The truth shall make you free" is no mere sentiment. When truth is more nearly approximated in action there is a tremendous gain in strength as well as a liberation. Although a long war also clears away some social, economic and political errors, it is not very effective for this purpose because the angers and hatreds of war tend strongly to becloud the truth, as has been clearly shown by the propaganda of two world wars and the present cold war.

Possibly to some readers this whole chapter may seem to be a structure of untried theory. Who in this actual world of hard realities does or ever would for an instant fear this so-called weapon of nonviolent resistance?

The answer is known to every student of history, every detective, secret-service man or C.I.D. officer, every really "hard-boiled" ruthless executive of an American industrial corporation which has had a strike of employees, every American trade union leader, every leader of a subject people striving for political freedom. The answer is that every "blood and iron" type of governor fears nonviolent resistance so much that he secretly hires *agents provocateurs* who go among the nonviolent resisters pretending to be of them, and invite them to deeds of violence or actually throw bombs or do deeds of violence themselves. This was the method of the Tsarist government of old Russia. The rulers in power immediately make great outcry, stir up public indignation against the "miscreants," call out the police or soldiery, and "repress the uprising" with considerable brutality, meanwhile assuring the world that these are stern but necessary steps taken only in the interests of public safety, law and order. Those striving for freedom or more privileges are indeed often violent in the first

instance. But if they are not violent, their opponents or the under-
lings of their opponents frequently stir up violence in order to take advantage of the public reaction against it. That they feel they need
to adopt such tactics shows how much they fear nonviolent resistance.

Nonviolent resisters must face this fact without anger or bitterness.
It is simply one item in the whole situation with which they have to
contend. Their defense is to build up a thorough discipline of nonviolence in feeling, thought, word and deed within each one of
their members. They must see the whole meaning of what they are
trying to do. They are trying to discipline and control the emotion
of anger and the instinct of pugnacity in the same way and to the
same extent that military discipline controls the emotion of fear and
the instinct of flight. Therefore, under this new discipline, violent
words and actions directed against the opponent or his interests are
to be made as traitorous to the cause as desertion is in the army. Anger
is as disgraceful and socially reprehensible among nonviolent resisters
as cowardice is among schoolboys or soldiers.

Once that understanding, attitude and discipline are attained among
the group of nonviolent resisters, any *agent provocateur* who comes
whispering among them or preaching violence, retaliation or revenge
will be immediately known for what he is and repudiated. And the
group will soon prove its tactics so clearly to the public that the latter
ter will not be deceived by the act of an *agent provocateur* bomb-
thrower or inflammatory speaker.

"But," says the shrewd critic, "even if we grant the efficiency of
this new weapon provided it could once get under way, would it not
quickly be rendered impossible merely by the killing, imprisonment
or deportation for life of the few leaders who understand it and see
its possibilities?"

The answer, outside countries ruled by Communists, again is No.
The idea has already gone too far. Before long, new leaders would
appear and new attempts be made. The success of nonviolence in
India was so dramatic and widely heralded that it is being tried again
in several countries. There is the success in the bus boycott by the
Negro community at Montgomery, Alabama, and its continuing use by
non-whites in South Africa. It will probably be used increasingly in
America in movements for economic and social justice not aimed
against the government. In North America there is enough knowledge

about Gandhi's ideas and work to create wide sympathy for any groups who sincerely use this method to gain justice. Public opinion will support such use in enough cases to promote the prestige and further success of the method.

Its use by black Africans and Indians in South Africa, while not yet successful, has won respect in most other parts of the world. There is a fair probability that it will be used by the black peoples of other parts of colonial Africa. Ghana, the new member of the British Commonwealth in West Africa, won its freedom in 1957 after a ten-year nonviolent struggle. Its leader, Kwame Nkrumah, in his autobiography says explicitly that the campaign for freedom was "based on the principle of absolute nonviolence as used by Gandhi in India," and "We repudiate war and violence."[22] The campaign was actually so carried out. Futhermore, he says explicitly that he intends to help the peoples of other parts of Africa to attain their freedom from colonial status, exploitation and social inequalities by this method. There is evidence of inconsistency in the use of the principle in Ghana and India but this is natural in the learning of any deeply new method.

There is some danger of thought control being so widely and deeply persuasive in America by means of radio, television, movies and newspapers that any movement for nonviolent resistance might be smothered. Though prophecy is risky for anyone, my guess, for what it may be worth, is that such complete thought control would fail. I think the method of nonviolence will prove so successful in many different situations that it will gather great momentum, understanding, confidence and prestige. Exploited groups suffering injustice everywhere will want to try it.

As for countries under Communist rule, they all want industrialization. That involves education, especially in science. The reasoning of modern science, especially physics, is contrary to the teachings of Marx and Lenin in regard to the primacy of matter. Modern science and money will, I believe, undermine Marxism. Communism, like everything else in the world, is changing, and one of the changes is a weakening of dogmatism and cruelty and persecution. As Louis Fischer has noted, the quiet heroism of Boris Pasternak in writing and publishing *Doctor Zhivago* and his behavior since then have apparently won the respect of the Russian government. The changes will accelerate, like all other changes in all countries.

It may be argued that nonviolent resistance would fail if attempted against armies of certain nations with a reputation for ruthlessness and callous brutality. Undoubtedly in such a case there would be losses, and perhaps heavy ones. The history of Cromwell's conquest of Ireland, and the record of the laws and punishments of those days shows clearly that the English in that century were fearfully brutal and callous, yet the nonviolent resistance of the Quakers prevailed against them. During the severe Nazi persecution and brutality toward German Jews just before 1940, the Nazi officials permitted American Quakers to do relief work in Germany because the Nazis remembered that, during the blockade and starvation of Germany by the British fleet just after World War I, American Quakers had brought food and much help and kindness to Germans then. Even Nazi hearts could be touched by long-continued kindness. When the Soviet government crushed the Hungarian rebellion in 1956, the morale of the Russian troops who had been stationed in Hungary and were used at first deteriorated so much in contact with the Hungarian workers that they had to be removed and replaced by troops from the Asian part of Russia. The latter believed, according to a U.N. report, that they were fighting French and British imperialists. Even Soviet indoctrination and discipline can be weakened. Barbarians respect courage, and are perhaps more easily subject to wonder and awe in the face of extraordinary events than are the more sophisticated or more highly organized nations.[23] Nonviolent resistance touches human nature itself, not merely its cultured areas. The psychological forces in nonviolent resistance operate in different ways against different nations, but they will operate effectively against them all, as surely as violent war has operated against them all.

Some people stand aghast at the thoroughness of the discipline of certain nations or classes, and think that such a factor could not be overcome by nonviolent resistance. The answer is that the truths of nonviolence are deeper than those of violence and affect human nature more profoundly and powerfully. More specifically, the reason for this greater effectiveness of nonviolent discipline is as follows. We have noted earlier that Napoleon stated that in war the relative importance of the moral elements to the physical elements is as three is to one. Captain B. H. Liddell Hart, a renowned British authority on military strategy and military history, has stated that in modern war (he was referring to war without nuclear weapons) the relative importance of the moral to the physical is as six is to one. Since in nonviolent resistance the modes of action and the appeal and influence are so completely and consistently moral in nature, whereas in war there are great moral inconsistencies and failures, the probability is strong that gentle resisters, if well-disciplined, can overcome forces that no violent army can handle. Therefore it is possible and not too difficult for believers in nonviolence to devise and practice a discipline which is still more thorough and profound, still more in accord with a wider range of subtle powers, and therefore still more powerful than the discipline of violent nations.

But to many it may seem that rarely in the history of the world has morality been at a lower ebb than now, and therefore it would be a huge mistake to rely on a purely moral appeal. Yet although there have been recently and still are dreadful cruelties and other violations of moral law practiced in the world, nevertheless there has never been such clear, strong recognition on the part of the holders of power of the importance of public opinion. It is shown both by the vast amounts of propaganda and by the secrecies and direct and indirect censorships practiced by governments, press, radio and television. In virtually every country in the world, incessant attempts are being made to put at least an appearance of justice, democracy and rightness on all public deeds. So moral laws are still strong and firm and persuasive. The vast sufferings of the modern world have made the consciences of all men more sensitive. I grant there is great apathy, but that has always been present.

To some it might seem that, in a war where the two parties had two very different socio-political theories and values (e.g., those of Marxism and capitalism), nonviolent resistance could not be an effective defense for either party. Suppose, for instance, the Soviet Union were violently attacking the United States but neither side used nuclear weapons; could the Americans successfully defend themselves and their institutions and way of life by using nonviolent resistance against the Russians? Obviously in that instance no form of defense could be successful until a large majority of Americans sincerely believed in it, a considerable number were well disciplined in it, and the nation had made most of its way of life consistent with that mode of defense. In such a case the Americans could not by nonviolent resistance successfully defend and maintain the faults and defects of capitalism—and there are some faults of capitalism since all forms of society have defects. Yet to the extent that American capitalism is consistent with human unity and kindness to everyone regardless of race, nation, religious belief or technical advance, it could survive by using nonviolent defense. Where it fails in those respects, it would have to abandon them or be defeated. If anyone wants to retain his faults as well as his virtues, he deserves defeat. The above argument is just as valid the other way around—if the United States were violently to attack Russia and Russia were to use nonviolent resistance.

Some people do not see how nonviolent resistance could possibly be effective against bombing from the air. Usually such bombing has not and probably would not be used unless the people of the bombed place had themselves used violence or were part of a nation engaged in violent warfare. In such a city there would of course be deaths and destruction of property from such bombing, just as if it were actively using anti-aircraft guns. But such bombing does not last indefinitely. It is followed by some sort of contact and parley. At that time the elements of nonviolence begin to operate. The continuance during World War II of life in Malta, Chungking, Hamburg and Berlin, and its return to Hiroshima and Nagasaki is evidence that in a non-nuclear limited war such bombing does not end all resistance.

Skeptics might assert that the advent of hydrogen and atom bombs and rocket missiles make the idea of nonviolent resistance against the governments of the United States, Russia and Great Britain completely nonsensical. And if other governments develop or acquire such bombs or rockets, there could be no nonviolent resistance against them either. All such governments would thereby, it could be alleged, become immune to this method and therefore it is silly to propose its use in those countries.

But the chances of any government using small "tactical" nuclear bombs against their own civilians is extremely small. Even the ruthless Soviet government did not use them against the East German or Hungarian rebels in 1953 and 1956. Such weapons are somewhat of a boomerang since the radioactivity generated by them contaminates a considerable area against those using them as well as against the opponents.

7

AN EFFECTIVE SUBSTITUTE FOR WAR

DESPITE THE HORRORS, futilities and destructiveness of war, there are nevertheless certain virtues and truths associated with it which humanity canot afford to lose. In any discussion of new ways of settling conflicts, these military virtues cannot safely be disregarded.

Before the First World War, the romance and glamor of war was an undoubted fact, especially for those who never had taken part in war. The two world wars have destroyed all the glamor. Yet there is in all hearts a desire to live a significant life, to serve a great idea and sacrifice oneself for a noble cause, to feel the thrill of spiritual unity with one's fellows and to act in accordance therewith. We all wish for strenuous action and the exercise of courage and fortitude, to be carried away by the enthusiasm of daring. We all love to undergo a common discipline and hardship for the sake of a fine ideal; to be in good effective order; to be strong, generous and self-reliant; to be physically fit, with body, mind and soul harmoniously working together foɪ a great purpose, thus becoming a channel of immense energies. Under such conditions, the whole personality is alert, conscious, unified and living profoundly, richly and exaltedly. Then one can be truly and gloriously happy. Martial music suggests many of these elements and their consequent exhilaration and exaltation.

Probably war and conflict seem to promise such results partly because our ordinary life of alleged peace is so often dull, trivial, monotonous and devoid of fine purpose. It is so full of frustration, resentments, balked disposition, hidden violence, oppression, pettiness and meanness; so insipid, fragmentary, full of cross-purposes and evil.

"Such a hopeless snarl, Anything to be relieved of such a mess!"

So cries the heart. Yet what a risk, to wrench ourselves from established life.

One reason why we take such deep delight in risk attending the search for this release is that such adventures may turn possibilities into accomplished facts. They are modes of creation, of "free activity of the soul," as Clausewitz says. Hence, after men have long been chained to an industrial routine, feeling themselves helpless cogs in a vast machine, the call of an immeasurable risk cannot easily be resisted. But war is attractive not merely for its orderly action and sense of unity for a great purpose; it also has solid elements of truth and virtue.

The most outstanding virtue of violence is that of courage. But violence is not the only occasion or test or proof of courage.

Another virtue is energy. All the deep emotions, especially fear and anger, are generators of tremendous energy. To be a channel of immense energy gives one a thrill and a satisfaction that can never be forgotten. Fear, anger and hatred are doubtless evil, but the energy that they arouse is, by itself, good; for as William Blake said, energy is divine.

Furthermore, the sincerity of many fighters and warriors is admirable. They live and work, sacrifice and die for their vision of the truth, even though they may be too inarticulate to express it in words. The militarist's vision of truth may be partial and cloudy, but he nevertheless lives, suffers and dies for the truth as he sees it. He may even be inspired by hatred, anger, and revenge, and may put his whole faith in material weapons, but he is true to himself and the faith that is in him. That much is fine and solid.

Another virtue of the militarists which deserves our admiration is discipline. Discipline establishes and maintains effective habits, creates solidarity and reliability, promotes self-respect and elicits respect from others.

The militarist is right when he says that conflict is an inevitable part of life. This world is inherently diverse and changing, and since human beings differ so much in the values they hold, in environment, inheritance, intelligence, tolerance and unselfishness, and are so bound by tradition and habit, the adjustments involved in change and growth necessarily result in conflicts. No strong or sensible person would want to abolish growth or change or the positive achievements that often issue from struggle. Struggle is a part of the very meaning of life.

These, then, seem to be the important virtues of the violent fighter: enterprise, courage, strenuous action, and endurance; sincerity, devotion and a sense of unity with one's own kind; order, training and discipline. His truth that conflict is inevitable is another element of his strength.

All these virtues and truths of war are given full scope and exercise in the nonviolent method of settling great disputes. If any nation or group adopts mass nonviolent resistance, no moral losses will result.

Walter Lippmann, in an excellent article on "The Political Equivalent of War," quotes from William James' essay, "The Moral Equivalent of War,"[1] and continues:

> "It is not sufficient to propose an equivalent for the military virtues. It is even more important to work out an equivalent for the military methods and objectives. For the institution of war is not merely an expression of the military spirit. It is not a mere release of certain subjective impulses clamoring for expression. It is also—and, I think, primarily—one of the ways by which great human decisions are made. If that is true, then the abolition of war depends primarily upon inventing and organizing other ways of deciding those issues which hitherto have been decided by war. . . .
>
> "Any real program of peace must rest on the premise that there will be causes of dispute as long as we can foresee, and that those disputes have to be decided, and that a way of deciding them must be found which is not war."[2]

"A way of deciding them which is not war." Is that way nonviolent resistance? Closer examination shows that it satisfies Lippmann's requirements. Nonviolent resistance not only utilizes the military virtues; it uses also on a moral plane many of the military methods and principles; it employs many of the same psychological processes; and it even retains some of the military objectives, with moral modifications. Military men know much about human nature, but nonviolent resisters know still more. If war has been in the past a practical method of making great human decisions, of settling great disputes, this new method will be still more effective for such a purpose.

The very principles of military strategy operate in this new mode of struggle.

Clausewitz's principles of war have been summarized by a British writer as follows:

> "Retaining the initiative, using the defensive as the decisive form of action, concentration of force at the decisive point, the determination of that

point, the superiority of the moral factor to purely material resources, the proper relation between attack and defense, and the will to victory."[3]

Other authorities state them somewhat differently, Foch, for instance, laying more stress on the offensive.

We have seen that the nonviolent resister begins an entirely new line of conduct. He seizes and maintains the moral initiative. He uses the principle of surprise most effectively. Clausewitz said: "Surprise plays a much greater part in strategy than in tactics; it is the most powerful element of victory,"[4] and a long line of military authorities agree.

The surprise of nonviolent resistance is effective partly because it is startling and partly because the opponent is so bound by his violent habits that he is ill-prepared to utilize the new tactics himself. He is like a wrestler using European methods pitted against a Japanese using jiu-jitsu. The surprise of nonviolent resistance, unlike that of war, is not due to deceit or stratagem but simply to its novelty and daring.

Napoleon stated,

"'It is an approved maxim in war, never to do what the enemy wishes you to do, for this reason alone, that he desires it. A field of battle, therefore, which he has previously studied and reconnoitred, should be avoided, and double care should be taken where he has had time to fortify and entrench. One consequence deducible from this principle is, never to attack a position in front which you can gain by turning."[5]

Nonviolent resistance acts fully in accord with Napoleon's principle. Your violent oponent wants you to fight in the way to which he is accustomed. If you utterly decline, and adopt a method wholly new to him, you have thus gained an immediate tactical advantage.

In "using the defensive as the decisive form of action," the peaceful resister in his external actions agrees with Clausewitz and Liddell Hart, but in respect to his psychological energies he agrees with Foch; he is constantly "attacking," that is, energetically seeking the psychological road for a truly satisfactory solution of the conflict. His energy is not used so much in opposition as in trying to open new, adequate and wise channels for the energies of both his opponents and himself to unite in and flow on together, and in removing defects from his own position. Nonviolent resistance is not directed against the *energy* of the opponent's desires but merely against their immediate direction, form or method. It seeks to discover for him a new and wiser channel for his energy.

This does not mean reducing the conflict to a tame debating society. Although sometimes a safe and easy issue of the conflict may be found, the nonviolent resister may feel assured of a fair probability that he will sooner or later have to suffer hardships and perhaps wounds, imprisonment and even death. If the struggle is against a powerful group, a corporation, a government or an established system of socio-economic beliefs, and is prolonged, the resisters may have to suffer a great deal. "War is hell," and in a long struggle soldiers and police may abandon all restraints. We assume that the peaceful resister is really in earnest, really believes in his cause, is ready to sacrifice for it, and is no more a coward than any soldier is. He must take risks. This is a real adventure, no parlor make-believe for pretenders or boasters.

But psychologically, nonviolent resistance differs in one respect from war. The object is not to make the opponent believe that he is crushed, but to persuade him to realize that he can attain practical security, or whatever else his ultimate desire may be, by easier and surer means than he saw formerly. The effort is furthermore to help him work out such new means, not rigidly or on any *a priori* plan, but flexibly in accordance with the deepest growing truth of the entire situation in all its bearings. Nonviolence does not destroy the opponent's courage, but merely alters his belief that his will and desire must be satisfied only in *his* way. Thus he is led to see the situation in a broader, more fundamental and far-sighted way, so as to work out a solution which will more nearly satisfy both parties in the light of a new set of conditions.

Does the nonviolent resister "concentrate his force at the decisive point," and is he active in "the determination of that point"? He certainly is. He decides, with Marshal Saxe, that "the secret of victory lies in the hearts of human beings"[6]—that is, that it is a matter of psychology. Therefore he concentrates upon the psychological forces in the situation, and deals with them as efficiently and powerfully as he possibly can. And in so far as concentration means bringing strength to bear against weakness, he does that also, for in this moral or psychological field he is far stronger and better prepared than his opponent.

We need not dilate further upon the belief and action of the non-violent resister, in respect to the principle of the "superiority of the moral factor to purely material resources." He acts more consistently and completely upon that principle than any soldier could.

"The proper relation between attack and defense" has been very searchingly considered by the peaceful resister. He knows that the best relation of all between these two energies is not one of opposition but of resolution, integration and sublimation. He thus enables both sides to win, and conquers both his own possible short-sightedness of aim and that of his enemy at the same time. The result is not a triumphant victor on the one side and a despondent, repressed vanquished on the other. Both sides are happy in the joint victory of their better selves and the common defeat of their mistakes.

Does the peaceful resister have the "will to conquer" which Foch calls "the first condition of victory"?[7] He surely does. Indeed, he must have an indomitable will to victory in order to endure the suffering put upon him. Moreover, he has a stronger incentive to win than has the ordinary soldier in war, for by this new way the final result is *sure* and settled permanently, and with a great release of energy and happiness for all concerned. There is no aftermath of resentment, hatred, bitterness, or revenge, no necessity for further threats or force.

There are other principles of strategy which also find parallels here —such principles as the economy of forces, the importance of information, mobility, endurance, etc.—but we need not discuss all of these. The similarities to the principles of military strategy are clear.

But the similarities between war and nonviolent resistance are not merely an interesting set of analogies. This entire chapter up to this point answers two doubts: namely, whether this method of struggle is not utterly foreign and new and suited only to Oriental peoples, and therefore whether it could be adopted by people with the modern Western attitude of mind. The facts that the military virtues are used and needed in this new form of struggle, and that the principles of military strategy apply here too, show that if we adopt this new mode of settling conflicts we will not be entirely reversing our previous experience, nor abandoning whatever true principles and values the human race may have garnered from its age-long experience of war. It may be that, for its first great mass success, nonviolent re-

sistance had to be used among a people who have much social awareness and who had been thoroughly inculcated and disciplined for
many centuries with ideas of nonviolence, as the Indians with their
Buddhist, Jain, and Hindu traditions have been. But after its first success, a desire to try it has risen in other countries, and its rationale is
coming to be understood. For obvious reasons, their desire and understanding will increase. Given desire and understanding, the courage,
organizing ability, and disciplinary capacity of other peoples, whether
Asian, African or Western, is not less than that of Indians. Hence the
use of the method may be expected to spread. The new method is an
advance, an improvement in the art of deciding public disputes, but
not so utterly foreign as to be unworkable by other peoples. By fully
understanding these relationships between war and nonviolent resistance we may provide ourselves an assurance with which we may
advance to this new procedure.

In cases where Asians and Africans have tried to relieve themselves of the economic and military pressure of European domina-
tion, they have complained that the West cannot understand any
language but that of force. If that is true, it means that the West will
be utterly unprepared and helpless in the face of well-disciplined,
thoroughly organized and wisely led nonviolent resistance, especially if it is accompanied by an equally thorough temporary non-vindic-
tive economic boycott. The strategic principle of surprise would operate most dramatically and effectively. To use nonviolent resistance
against the West would be complying with Napoleon's Sixteenth
Maxim of War quoted above. But I am inclined to think that the
West will come to understand the new language fairly soon, once it
is shown to be strong language. Already there is a partial understanding of the new language, and considerable worry to boot. The grant
of freedom to Ghana by the British government is one instance of
this.

If, in some future conflict, both sides should use nonviolent resistance, that side would win which most deeply understood and was
best disciplined and prepared in this new method. That would be the
side which achieved the most self-purification, which attained the
most social truth and showed the finest love. It would thereby attain
the greater inner unity and strength, the greater respect from its opponents and the public.

In summary, we see that nonviolent resistance resembles war in these eight ways:

(1) It has a psychological and moral aim and effect,
(2) It is a discipline of a parallel emotion and instinct,
(3) It operates against the morale of the opponents,
(4) It is similar in principles of strategy,
(5) It is a method of settling great disputes and conflicts,
(6) It requires courage, dynamic energy, capacity to endure fatigue and suffering, self-sacrifice, self-control, chivalry, action,
(7) It is positive and powerful,
(8) It affords an opportunity of service for a large idea, and for glory.

It does not avoid hardships, suffering, wounds or even death. In using it men and women may still risk their lives and fortunes and sacrifice all. Nevertheless the possibilities of casualties and death are greatly reduced under it, and they are all suffered voluntarily and not imposed by the nonviolent resisters.

In the Indian struggle for independence, though I know of no accurate statistics, hundreds of thousands of Indians went to jail, probably not more than five hundred received permanent physical injuries, and probably not over eight thousand were killed immediately or died later from wounds. No British, I believe, were killed or wounded. Considering the importance and size of the conflict and the many years it lasted, these numbers are much smaller than they would have been if the Indians had used violence toward the British.

Nonviolent resistance is more efficient than war because it costs far less in money as well as in lives and suffering. Also it usually permits a large part of the agricultural and industrial work of the people to go on, and hence the life of the country can be maintained during the struggle.

It is again more efficient than war because "the legitimate object of war is a more perfect peace." If the peace after the war is to be better than that which preceded it, the psychological processes of the conflict must be such as will create a more perfect peace. You can't climb a mountain by constantly going downhill. Mutual violence inevitably breeds hatred, revenge and bitterness—a poor foundation for a more perfect peace. The method of nonviolent resistance, where there really is resistance, so as to bring all the issues out into the open, and the working out of a really new settlement, as nearly as possible in accord with the full truth of the issues at stake—this method does not leave a sense of frustration and it brings a more perfect peace.

Considering the completeness of its effects, nonviolent resistance is as quick and probably quicker than war. It is a weapon that can be used equally well by small or large nations or groups, by the economically weak and by the apparently strong, and even by individuals. It compels both sides and neutrals to seek the truth, whereas war blinds both sides and neutrals to the truth.

As we have already seen and will show further, nonviolent resistance certainly produces less ill-effects, if any, than war does, and this decrease of ill-effects applies to the users of nonviolence, to the opposing side, and to society and the world at large.

It is interesting to note that in early 1958 there was published a book by a British naval officer (not a pacifist), Commander Sir Stephen King-Hall, in which he argues that nonviolent resistance is now the best and only possible successful mode of defense of Great Britain against armed attack. He argues the points in detail and cogently: "We must," he says, "ask ourselves this question: 'If the contribution of violence (*i.e.,* military operations) to the settlement of differences of opinion or conflicts (*werre*) between sovereign states has evolved to such intensity that it is totally destructive, has not violence outlived its usefulness in disputes between large states?' It looks to me as if this is the truth. Bearing in mind that in major disputes violence has become equated with nuclear energy violence, I am forced to consider what possibilities are open to us if we exclude violence from our defense plans on the grounds that violence has become our master instead of our slave."[8] Many other keen thinkers all through the West agree that nuclear weapons have destroyed the effectiveness of war as a means to settle large disputes between nations.[9]

May we not then fairly describe nonviolent resistance as an effective substitute for war?

It is realistic in that it does not eliminate or attempt to eliminate possibilities of conflict and differences of interest, and includes *all* factors in the situation—both material and imponderable, physical and psychological. A British psychologist argues that the fundamental reasons for war are sadism and masochism, and that, until these deep-seated urges are modified, war cannot be ended.[10] In so far as sadism and masochism are perverted expressions of a desire for power, however, nonviolent resistance can control them by substituting its own method of securing a power that is much greater and more satisfying.

It does not require any nation to surrender any part of its real sovereignty or right of decision, as a world government might. It does not surrender the right of self-defense, although it radically alters the nature of the defense. It requires no expensive weapons or armament, no drill grounds or secrecy. It does not demoralize those who take part in it, but leaves them finer men and women than when the struggle began.

Moreover, the method does not require the machinery of a government or a large wealthy organization. It may be practiced and skill may be acquired in it in every situation of life, at home and abroad, by men and women of any and all races, nations, tribes, groups, classes or castes, young and old, rich and poor. That women take part in it is important. Indeed, they are more effective in it than most men.

Inasmuch as some of the elements involved are essentially the same as trust, they have the same energizing effect as financial credit, only more so. Thus it stimulates and mobilizes, during the conflict and for a long time thereafter, all the idealism and energy of all groups and parties.

It is much superior to William James' detailed suggestions in his essay on "The Moral Equivalent of War," in that it does not require state organization, direction or assistance; it is not used against the exterior forces and conditions of nature but against human wrongs and evils. It is therefore much more dramatic, interesting and alluring, both for young men and old, and for women, too. It has even more possibilities of high daring, adventure, risk, bravery, endurance, and truly fine and noble romance than any of the chivalrous violent fighting of bygone ages.

May we not therefore say of it in the words which Marshal Foch used in reference to a different occasion: "The new kind of war has begun, the hearts of soldiers have become a new weapon."[11]

8

NONVIOLENCE AND THE STATE

Nonviolent resistance is the key to the problem of liberty in the modern state. That seems like a large claim until we begin to reflect upon the part which force and compulsion play in all the relationships in which the state takes part.

All observers recognize that compulsion, intimidation and violence have been and still are a very large and perhaps predominating element in the state, and especially in political government.[1] If anyone feels inclined to dispute the scholars on this point, let him examine the figures showing that the expenditures for past and future wars form a very high percentage of the total expenditures of the governments of the great majority of nations. To this he should add the state expenditures for prisons, the administration of criminal law and a certain part of the administration of civil law. The state has many fine elements, but they perhaps do not counterbalance the large part played by force and compulsion.

This condition of affairs is due not to a particular ruling class, as the Communists would have us believe, but to an inner psychological attitude which prevails through all groups and classes in the so-called "civilized" world. The Marxians say that political forms and methods are determined chiefly by economic forces. We would say that both political and economic processes, at least in relation to violence and coercion, are due to still deeper psychological factors. The amount of coercion and violence in the state is a reflection or resultant of a similar tendency and attitude in all our life and activities, both individual and associative.

The nonviolent resister believes that a large part of the activities of the state are founded upon a mistake, namely, the idea that fear is the strongest and best sanction for group action and association. He believes that fear is divisive and therefore cannot be the foundation for permanent unity and strength. He believes that in the family and in education it has now been realized that fear is not a sound basis for action. There we find substituted the more positive and growth-stimulating forces of intellectual curiosity, wonder, love and cooperation. The nonviolent resister looks forward to a time when a similar realization will come in regard to the larger associations of states. He believes that nonviolent resistance will probably be an important means in reaching this realization.

The principles of nonviolent resistance can be applied to diplomacy as well as war, for the two are closely allied. "War" says Clausewitz, "is a part of political intercourse" and "only a continuation of state policy by other means."[2] Compared with war, nonviolent resistance is a safer and more effective instrument of policy. By its use, the entire military and naval expenses of all nations can be completely eliminated.

In so far as diplomacy has been characterized by secrecy and deceit, the principle of truth involved in nonviolent resistance will bring about reform. Secrecy and deceit are signs of fear, but nonviolent resistance proceeds upon the basis of control and eventual elimination of fear. It insists on truth and openness in all dealings. Gandhi's practice is a living embodiment of this principle.

Nonviolent resistance can be used internationally, with or without economic boycott as circumstances require. Causes that some people think cannot be submitted to arbitration may be handled by such means. Mere nonresistance alone will not do. There must be constructive resistance. The Indian Non-Cooperation Movement in 1922 gave an example which was promising.

Commander King-Hall points out that war is fundamentally a conflict of opinions. Victory, according to Marshal Saxe, is due to a change of opinions in the minds and hearts of the opponents. The struggle is fundamentally in the realm of ideas and moral principles, as Napoleon and other military writers have pointed out. Since it is axiomatic among all warriors that the best form of defense is to attack, then the most efficient attack is not in the realm of material weapons but in the realm of ideas, feelings and moral principles. I do not mean mere argument, though that is important, but still more by putting fine moral principles into action, by being strictly honest and candid with oneself as well as one's opponents, admitting one's past mistakes, first, unilaterally (every one of us has made mistakes), respecting one's opponents and showing it in deeds, being willing to yield something—even something big and valuable, provided it is not a principle—being kind and generous to the opponents, stopping all threats and harsh holding-fast to the right. This will be very difficult, a very high price to pay for peace. But with all the load of past moral mistakes everywhere, we cannot have peace unless we are willing to pay a high price.

If put into the context of a struggle against Communists, a fight for freedom for our way of life, we must remember that freedom is a by product of trust, mutual respect, honesty, nonviolence, tolerance, patience and actively expressed good will. The leaders of the nations must guide the people into such ways. Nonviolent resistance is the summation of them.

Attempts to improve international relations absorb the time, energy and money of many people. While I admire the devotion shown, most of it seems to me to be wasted because it deals with symptoms instead of the root of the trouble. It is like putting poultices on a cancer. War is an institution, and institutions are external expressions of previous inner attitudes and ways of thinking.[3] To try merely to alter the institution is like locking the barn door after the horse is stolen. Even the Mosaic commandment, "Thou shalt not kill," begins psychologically at the wrong end of the problem.

Peace, on the other hand, is not an institution. Like happiness and liberty, it cannot be had by direct effort. It is an indirect byproduct of other conditions, chief of which are mutual trust and a strong sense of the unity of mankind and its overriding importance. Trust, in turn, grows out of deeds that reveal continuing intelligence, good will and desire to cooperate and promote the common welfare. These underlying attitudes can be stimulated to grow. Their growth can be begun unilaterally. It is upon their development and growth that effort should be concentrated. Once they are strong and permanent, peace will come automatically.

World courts, leagues of nations, peace pacts and peace congresses do little toward improving the inner attitudes or psychological dispositions and habits of mind. Too many peacemakers work only on externals, and disregard deepseated inconsistencies and forces working for war in many parts of the economic, social, educational and organized religious systems. To say this is not to oppose their effort, but only to wish that it might be more efficient.

Inasmuch as peacemakers need to be especially sensitive to the truth, it seems desirable to present here two criticisms of their activity, for them to ponder. One was well phrased by Reinhold Niebuhr:

" . . . The implication is that England and America are the only two really solvent nations in the Western World, and that, since they have what they want and need, it is to their interest to preach peace. The hungry nations will meanwhile fail to react to this moral idealism. They will shrewdly and cynically observe that it is always the tendency of those who have to extol the virtue of peace and order and to place those who have not at a moral disadvantage.

"It is quite impossible for the strong to be redemptive in their relation to the weak if they are not willing to share the weakness of the weak, or at least to equalize in some degree the disproportion of advantages."[4]

Another incisive criticism is made by Trotsky in respect to a certain sort of "pacifism." He says that "a responsible function is allotted to pacifism in the economy of warfare." By this he refers to the pacifists who go around talking about "our sacred duty to do all in our power to preserve the nation from the horrors of war," yet always carefully adding, "If war should come, we will all support the government, of course." Trotsky proceeds:

" 'To do everything in our power against the war,' means to afford the voice of popular indignation an outlet in the form of harmless demonstration, after having previously given the government a guarantee that it will meet with no serious opposition, in the case of war, from the pacifist faction.

"Official pacifism could have desired nothing better. It could now give satisfactory assurance of imperialistic 'preparedness.' After Bryan's own declaration, only one thing was necessary to dispose of his noisy opposition to war, and that was, simply, to declare war. And Bryan rolled right over into the government camps. And not only the *petite bourgeoisie,* but also the broad masses of the workers, said to themselves: 'If our government, with such an outspoken pacifist as Wilson at the head, declares war, and if even Bryan supports the government in the war, it must be an unavoidable and righteous war.' "[5]

It is easy to see how that type of "pacifism" helps to rally the entire country to the support of militarists at the time they most need it. They are glad to let such "pacifists" throw a gentle moral glow over affairs before war and then fill themselves and the masses with moral fervor in support of war as soon as it comes.

International peace requires the development of a world community.[6] The mood of mutual tolerance, respect and good will needed for the establishment and operation of such a community will best be created, in social practice, by the use of nonviolent resistance for the righting of existing wrongs.

One weakness of most peace proposals is that they all expect the action to be taken by governments or large organizations, or at least someone other than the proponent. The advantage of nonviolent resistance is that it begins at home and can and needs to be practiced in all the small private relations between people as a preparation for and accompaniment of its use on a large scale. Nobody can dodge the responsibility for its success. The poorest and most insignificant can practice it as finely, successfully and usefully as prime ministers, presidents, financiers, labor leaders or other powerful persons. Through nonviolent resistance we can reach an active, reasoned belief in the conditions that result in peace, conditions capable of continuous practice in all grades of life and all sorts of conflict, so as to educate everyone into a conviction that they give better results, more efficiently, than violence.

The causes of disagreement and conflict between nations are legion, and need not be discussed here. Yet there is one group of causes so very important at present that it may not be out of place to consider it briefly. This is the economic and political relationship between nations of the temperate zone and those of the tropics, together with the international jealousies resulting therefrom between nations of the former group. I agree with Gandhi and Simone Weil that modern industrialism and much commerce are inherently exploitative and violent in spirit.[7] It is recognized now in Europe and America that diversified farming creates economic prosperity and stability for the farmer and reduces the likelihood of plant disease, insect pests, market gluts, and other risks. It also increases the yield per acre. Yet, at the same time, Europe and the United States are asking and compelling the tropics to develop large plantations and single crop agriculture, to raise in this way rubber, jute, cotton, hemp, sugar, tobacco, tea, coffee, rice, oil seeds, coconuts, bananas, oranges, pineapples, etc. By this "mining" of the land, the white man is passing a heavy burden onto the tropics, reducing their prosperity, depleting their soil, ultimately decreasing their productivity, increasing their losses from plant disease and insects, and market depressions.[8]

Some observers say that the present civilization and culture of the temperate zones is now largely based on tropical products, such as rubber, cotton, jute, vegetable oils, coffee, tea, tobacco, spices, petroleum oil, etc., and that the tropics must do their share of maintaining the other civilizations. Other observers point to the restless energy of inhabitants of the temperate zones and the relative lethargy of tropical peoples, and do not see, therefore, how exploitation of the tropics could be prevented even if it were desirable on other grounds. Still others believe that industrial nations ought to exploit the tropics in order to spread the blessings of industrialism over all humanity.

It is all very well to talk of the economic interdependence of the different nations, but to use that as a high-sounding excuse for the sort of exploitation that is now going on will not do. International trade is excellent, but every nation ought to do its utmost first to produce its own essential food and clothing—the bare necessities of its life as a nation. That policy is not now followed by the controlling financial, industrial and political groups of any nation in the Western world, though perhaps Denmark and one or two other small European countries are not far from it. A large amount of self-dependence for the essential necessities of national life is the economic basis of national self-respect, mutual international respect and a preventative of economic parasitism. Beyond and above that, let trade proceed as merrily as it can, but with a minimum of exploitation. And let each nation and each group within the nation use nonviolent resistance to keep its own minimum low and to educate the holders of power to make social use of it, and to keep them in that path.

Let us now consider the internal relationships of the state.

The upholders of the state sometimes assert that nonviolent resistance to the state or to a specific law is not only unlawful but promotive of anarchy. But democracy is a valid form of government and social order, and democracy is founded on the consent of the governed. The theory of democracy does not assert that that consent or refusal must or can be evidenced only by marks on pieces of paper, the ballot. Refusal of consent may be democratically evidenced by action, by nonviolent resistance together with willingness to go to jail for violation of the law. This form of resistance, together with suffering the penalty, is a mode of persuasion, an appeal to the moral sensitiveness of the governors and the people. Persuasion is also a part of the democratic process.

The group within each state toward which the state uses compulsory force most constantly is that of the criminals. It is therefore interesting to find that the attitude and methods of nonviolent resistance are the conclusions toward which all the experience of penology and the investigations of psychiatrists, criminologists and social reformers are steadily tending.[10]

If there is ever any reform after forceful punishment or imprisonment, it is not caused by the force or even the suffering. The change depends upon the reaction of the suffering person, and cannot take place unless there is stimulus to some latent or potential goodness in the criminal. Intelligent kindness is a far more effective stimulus than any force can be. If force were the true cause of rehabilitation, its efficacy would increase with repetition. But all experience shows that a repetition of force merely hardens the prisoner and stimulates a desire for revenge.[11]

Violence and severe punishment have proved unavailing for thousands of years. The facts compel us to admit that cruel punishment is not only ineffective but is injurious to prison wardens and guards and to society as well as to the criminal. Also we now know that society is itself responsible for many of the conditions that create criminals. Nonviolent, loving, curative methods are the only ones that work or can possibly work. This means careful psychiatric examinations and psychiatric treatment; remedial diet;[12] medical care if need be; training in a useful craft or occupation; wise general education, good food, good quarters; decent, kindly, respectful treatment; many sorts of stimuli and opportunities for normal expression and living; wise probation; good juvenile and delinquent courts. The criminal courts should have only the function of deciding whether or not the crime has been committed and the accessory facts. They should have no power of punishment. Thereafter the case should be handled by physicians, psychiatrists, psychologists,[13] social workers, teachers, and employment agencies. The object should be not to make good prisoners but to make criminals into good citizens.

There are, of course, many dangerous and probably incurable criminals at present who require close restraint. They are the inevitable product of existing defective familial and social processes and penal systems. They will not disappear nor will they cease to be produced until society itself is changed for the better. Prison reform and criminal reform are parts of general social and economic reform.

But when really sound treatment is given the criminals and when society steps forward in its own reform, the prison population will greatly decrease. Even the feebleminded and insane are capable of great improvement by proper treatment. Sound diet alone has worked wonders in numerous cases.

In the chapters on the psychology of nonviolent resistance we stated that imitation and suggestion are most powerful when unconscious or subconscious. It is known that drunken people are very suggestible, and that in many types of insanity the subconscious is peculiarly alert and sensitive. Many insane people seem to have an uncanny faculty of perceiving the real purposes of those with whom they come in contact. This type of sensitiveness may prevail also in certain types of delirium.

This suggests that real nonviolent kindness is a language which many cases of delirium, insanity, drunkenness and crime would understand and respond to in more instances than is ordinarily believed. Certain specific occasions where nonviolence was successful in handling such cases confirm this conclusion.[14] Good music, especially participation in well-trained choral singing, has been found in at least one prison to exercise a profound and lasting beneficial influence on many criminals. Probably there are countless other unrecorded instances. Doubtless there are certain types of mental degeneracy where the nervous integrations are so badly injured that they are incapable of making any response in kind to nonviolent treatment. But they may be few, and capable of unmistakable diagnosis and description.

It would be desirable for criminologists, psychiatrists and physicians to make a long and careful study of all types of crime, mental disease or disability in relation to the possibility and desirability of handling them by wholly nonviolent or non-forceful methods. Too much is now left to the haphazard experience and hasty generalizations of wardens, nurses and attendants. Carefully worked-out information codified into rules and made a subject of intelligent instruction would be of immense assistance to prisons, houses of correction, reform schools, hospitals, mental hospitals, private nurses, policemen and physicians. But before these can be put into effect, a majority of citizens must give up their belief in and desire for punishment and revenge and the idea that the threat of violent punishment is an effective deterrent to crime.

The use of such rules would serve to increase considerably the respect and affection of many people for government and corrective and remedial institutions, and help also in the prompter reform and cure of many criminals and patients. By careful study it will be possible, I am confident, to reduce the amount and frequency of forcible restraint very considerably. What we need is a sincere, persistent, intelligent effort to eliminate it entirely—to regard every obstacle thereto as an indication of our ignorance of human nature rather than as an inherent impossibility of any kind.

Violent defense against thieves and burglars arises out of our ideas about property and the true nature of the self. Most killings by thieves and other criminals are not strictly "in cold blood," but out of fear that the victim will somehow harm the criminal. If the threatened victim is wholly unafraid, friendly, kind, generous and imaginative, there is relatively small chance of his receiving physical injury.[15]

Such considerations indicate that it will be eventually possible and practicable to forego violent defense of property. It is a part of the duty of nonviolent resisters to help bring about such a state of affairs. It will be for mankind as a whole a slow process, but there is no reason why the progress should not be steady and sometimes, and in some places, rapid.

It is interesting to realize that nonviolent resistance can be used both by the state and the prisoners. If the state considers itself the injured party and the criminal the attacker, it can offer him nonviolent reformatory treatment. If the criminal is mentally competent and feels that really he is the victim of an unjust social system and brutal wardens and police, he too may offer nonviolent resistance and do his share toward prison reform. In this connection, Gandhi's instructions for the jail conduct of political prisoners are of interest, though we have not space to quote them here.[16]

In some instances where innocent men have been sentenced to long imprisonments and even death, there has been much severe criticism directed against the governors, judges and other officials involved. This seems to me a waste of energy based on a misconception of the real forces at work. The fault does not lie with the men in office. The real causes are psychological and spiritual, and it is these and this institutionalized form that must be resisted and transformed. Governments are the external results of inner concepts and attitudes. They are the institutionalized forms of our habitual inner attitudes and ideas. Each one of us is partly responsible. The re-education must be directed primarily at this foundation, though, of course, it should find expression in all situations and relationships.

The police system also needs constant modification in the direction of less violence. Certain police functions are necessary in any complex modern society—such as directing traffic in city streets, providing information for strangers, helping to settle altercations without violence, helping lost children, directing large crowds, providing a disciplined orderly nucleus of leaders and helpers in times of public disaster such as fires, floods, earthquakes, severe storms, epidemics of disease, etc. Even after the advantages of nonviolence become widely recognized, there will still be people whose habits of violence persist, whose self-control is poor, or who will still occasionally hope to gain their ends by violence. For a generation or two after such recognition, it may be necessary to permit the police to use a greatly restricted amount of physical compulsion in certain cases where physical violence has already been used or overtly threatened by some other person. Long experience in England indicates that under such circumstances probably no firearms, sticks or brutality would be needed. Certainly, strong efforts should be made to stop most police violence immediately and eliminate all police violence as rapidly as we can educate society to nonviolence and eradicate the conditions which create violent crime. The policeman of the future, by his example and leadership in firm, intelligent, strong, creative kindness, can do much to educate the masses to nonviolence as a part of daily routine life. It is in this direction, one hopes, that police systems will evolve, and indeed they must so evolve if we are ever to create a truly sound political order.

9

PERSUASION

THE FOREGOING CHAPTERS may have made nonviolent resistance seem plausible. Yet many people who read them will still be skeptical of its effectiveness, despite the fact that, under Gandhi's leadership, it won freedom for India. The European mass persecutions, the use of atom and hydrogen bombs, the worldwide bloodshed, destruction, starvation, ruthless cruelties, and horrors of all sorts during the past two or three decades give pause to anyone. One's hopes are halted not only by the vastness of the devilment but also by its thoroughness.

Would highly disciplined and wholly determined aggressors ever be stopped by deeds of kindly persuasion? Could the holders of ultimate political and economic power really be persuaded to yield up their power by the use of nonviolent resistance? The history of mankind is so full of selfishness, greed, violence and cruelty that the possibility of improvement often seems doubtful. The power of entrenched interests is so immense and the energy of organized aggression is so tremendous that it is very difficult to see how gentle resistance plus love could either effectively sap such power or overcome or divert such energy. The destruction of both ponderables and imponderables by modern military weapons is so terrific that it is hard to believe that the power of slow-acting, slight or gentle forces can be superior. Are pacifists only naïve builders of false utopias?

In nature, the most important forces are silent. Examples are gravitation, sunlight, electro-magnetic forces, bacteria, the growth processes of plants and animals, the effects of environment. A considerable portion of material forces, such as gravitation, magnetism, heat, electric waves and sub-molecular forces, are invisible even under the microscope. Most of these forces, except by their results, are unperceivable by man's sense of touch. A large number of important foci of energies, such as enzymes, yeasts, cells, genes, hormones, vitamins, electrons and protons, are exceedingly small. The operations of many of the forces essential to human life are relatively slow and are cumulative in their effects. Instances are the building of soil on which all land life depends, the warming up each spring of the soil and air in temperate climes, the full maturing of human beings, the flowering of a civilization. Many forces which mold human beings, as for example the use of symbols or the desire for social status, are exceedingly subtle, to be appreciated and used only by the most observant. Yet what potent controls these two forces have been in the history of persons, villages and empires!

In many cases, exceedingly small forces can and do markedly influence vastly larger systems or organisms. Necessity to save space prevents me from citing instances. I can only refer the reader to a good encyclopedia, the articles on surface tension, hormones, enzymes, smell, trace elements, and catalysts.[1] The ability of exceedingly small quantities to alter a relatively large system can be proved in that branch of mathematics called differential equations.

The ability of a minute force to alter a system which by comparison is very large is most frequently and clearly seen where the large system is complex or delicately balanced. The human body is such a complex and delicately balanced set of forces and, as we know in the instance of hormones, the entire bodily poise, development, health and control is altered by the hormones in exceedingly small quantities. This is also true of the psychic aspect of man. Such subtle entities as hopes, with no apparent basis in fact, will guide and sustain a person or a nation through years of effort or endurance. Think, for example, how the hopes of the Jews have buoyed them up through millenniums of political subjection. Society is a system of many complex forces in mobile equilibrium, and at various times the balance is delicate. It is subject therefore to alteration by minute forces.

In other instances, the tiny forces affect the great mass by an accumulation. Stimuli far below what is called "the threshold of response," when sufficiently repeated, may cause an accumulative "staircase effect," often quite powerful.[2]

Thus, many of the most important forces are not perceivable by our crude human senses. Aside from their ultimate results, those forces in themselves are not dramatic or adequately appreciated by the majority of mankind. The connection between these imponderable forces and their ultimate effects is often so subtle or distant or slow that we fail to understand the originating forces. Yet, despite the slowness of human recognition, these forces are nonetheless real and powerful. Radio waves, for example, have always been present in storms, but man learned about them only within the last 85 years. Those who come to appreciate and understand such subtle forces can put them to human use with immeasurable benefit.

Such a slight and subtle but immensely powerful force is the combination of loving-kindness and nonviolent resistance.

A great number of biological experiments have shown that living animals respond in one way or another to many kinds of stimuli. Such stimuli may be mechanical, electrical, thermal, chemical, light, changes of atmospheric pressure, changes of humidity of surrounding air, smells, food intake, work, glandular secretions, infections, drugs, emotions, and in man, sentiments and thoughts. These researches have also shown that the responses affect one or more of practically all the stimulated animal's organs, tissues or functions, and that the responses occur in phases.[3] There are different kinds of phases. A one-phase or monophase response is in one direction only, say a continuous increase in activity of some sort. A dual phase or biphasic effect is first one kind of reaction and then after a while a reversal to a reaction of just the opposite kind. Cocaine, for instance, in a dilution of 1:1000, first constricts the blood vessels of a frog and then dilates them.

Kotschau showed in a wealth of experiments[4] that all responses of living tissues to stimuli could be grouped as follows: a slight stimulus will produce a weak monophasic response; a medium-strength stimulus causes a double-phasic response which has a stronger effect at the beginning, followed by a reversal; while a strong stimulus or a very large dose causes a short, intense effect followed by irreversible injury. As an example of Kotschau's rule, Tanaka found that a small amount of adrenalin put into the bloodstream of an animal shortens the time of clotting of blood, and this shortening effect continues; a moderate amount of adrenalin at first lengthens the blood-clotting time and then shortens it; while a large quantity of adrenalin at first shortens the blood-clotting time and then destroys the clotting ability permanently.

Experience as well as laboratory experiment indicates that the stimuli which cause animal organisms to grow are slight, causing a reaction of the monophasic type, and must be many times repeated. Medical experience also indicates that in general the drug stimuli which most effectively and without harmful reactions restore a sick organism to health are also slight, causing a one-phase response without reversal.[5]

Consider the bearing of these observations on our subject.

The believer in nonviolence does not assume with Rousseau that all persons at the beginning of their lives are inherently good, nor with Calvin that they are inherently and continuously sinful with only sporadic aspirations or goodness. He assumes that each person has inherently all the time both capacities, for good and for evil. Both potentialities are plastic. Which capacity will develop and how far it will develop depends on which one is frequently stimulated to cause growth. The vast amount of evil in history has been largely due to the kinds of stimuli to which man has allowed himself to be subject. So the believer in nonviolence assumes, on the basis of what seems to be sound historical and psychological evidence that, except for a few congenital mental defectives, every person has in him some tiny spark or potentiality of goodness. This is true no matter how encrusted that potentiality may be with habitual pride, prejudice, hatred, callousness, cruelty, or criminality.[6]

Thus the faith of the nonviolent resister in the ultimate flowering of the good potentialities of all people is not a blind or naïve faith. It has a solid foundation in the above-described intrinsic quality of all living protoplasm—the fact that all living organisms respond to stimuli, and that in the more complex organisms the responses are adapted to the stimuli so as to tend to preserve the species. Adaptation to environment is the large-scale proof of this. In the most complex and delicately balanced organisms, such as man, the response tends to partake of the same quality as the stimulus.

Moreover, as we have already seen, responses are called forth by exceedingly small stimuli, such stimuli as in the moral field would be called gentle.

This principle of stimulus and response also acts upon man's intellectual faculties. All education is based on this fact—and indeed so is the growth of civilizations. We assume, for example, that every child has a potential capacity for mathematics. We subject the child to many repetitions of the gentle stimulus of solving mathematical problems in school, the problems increasing in difficulty day after day. After eight or ten years of development under that regime, the child can easily solve mathematical problems which to Plato and Aristotle, the wisest men of ancient Greece, were utterly impossible. Part of the advance is due to improved mathematical notation, but much also to thorough use of suitable stimuli. The process of stimulus and response can likewise immensely enhance man's emotional and moral faculties.

Thus, growth in response to gentle, appropriate and sufficiently repeated stimuli is a sure thing, surer and more enduring than any form of political government, any economic action, or any military campaign. It is as sure as the fact that there is life on this planet. It can be relied upon without any hesitation or doubt.

Dictatorships cannot long grow or endure, because in them the stimuli are not gentle and so are incompatible with the inherent process of growth. That which cannot grow cannot adapt itself, and so cannot endure in this modern world of rapid social changes.

Thus the believer in nonviolence is convinced that, because the potentiality for good exists in every living person, the potentiality itself is living, is therefore subject to the law of stimulus and response, and hence is capable of growth until, compared with the harmful living factors in any given person, it becomes as strong, or even stronger. This, I think, is what Jesus meant when he told his disciples to forgive seventy times seven—repeating many, many times the gentle stimulus to unity implied by forgiveness.

The believer in nonviolence is also convinced from the examples in nature that the potentialities for goodness which are in a group, a corporation or a nation can by suitable stimuli be made to grow beyond their potentialities for evil. The law of stimulus and response applies as much to a forest as to a single tree, to the actions of a herd of elephants as to the actions of one elephant. Among human beings a collective does not have initiative. That has to be supplied by individuals. A human collective, however, may have more versatility and intellectual range than an individual, and by means of suitable organization and discipline, groups are capable of highly moral actions and reactions. Examples are found in the various struggles by nonviolent resistance under Gandhi's leadership. Disciplined groups of several thousand people, mostly peasants, stood up to attacks by police with clubs, or to gunfire by soldiers, yet maintained complete nonviolence and mostly did not run. Other examples are the building of European cathedrals and the growth of consumers' cooperatives.

The statement that human collectives are less moral than the individuals which compose them is a highly doubtful generalization. The ability of a human collective to behave morally depends on such factors as the extent and duration of its organization, the structure of the organization, its size and the sizes of any component subgroups in it, the interrelationships of the subgroups and the kind of integration among them, the kind of discipline (if any) to which the members have been subject, the duration of that discipline, the clarity of the ideas of the group and the extent of their permeation among the members, the extent and clarity of understanding of the group's purposes among its members, the loftiness of the common ideal, the simplicity or complexity of their general purpose, the quality of leadership, and the moral character of the environment. With so many variables as these, the broad generalization of the immorality of all human collectives is not valid. It disregards too much pertinent evidence. It does not square with the results of a wealth of patient and careful biological experiments and observations.[7]

Some of the doubts about the efficacy of nonviolence are due to overlooking the necessity, in most cases, for many repetitions of the gentle stimulus, and forgetting that this takes time. We may learn also that in order to bring best results the stimuli need to be spaced in a certain rhythm. Everybody realizes that a war is made up of many, many skirmishes and battles, but plenty of nonviolent resisters seem to expect this other kind of struggle to be successful and finished in short order. If success is not prompt, they get badly discouraged. The lack of immediate victory does not prove the inefficiency of the method. The discouragement proves only a failure to understand the process. Those same people realize that, in order to become a physician, a person must go through eight years of grammar school, four years of high school, four years of college, four years of medical school, and sixteen to eighteen months of hospital internship—in all, twenty-five or twenty-six years of preparation. And success in the profession can come only after at least five more years of work. All that time is generally considered well spent. Yet in India and elsewhere some critics called the method of nonviolence folly only a few years before independence was achieved, because the teaching of it to a nation of 400,000,000 people had won only partial advance after an effort lasting twenty-five years. That struggle for political freedom took twenty-eight years.[8]

If freedom is worth anything, it is worth fifty or a hundred years of unstinted effort in rigid adherence to the method. The use of this nonviolent method leads to steady improvement, while the use of violence gives a double-phase result, with a reversal and ultimate loss of what at first may seem to be won. It should be realized that in India each time a large-scale collective application of the method was used—in 1920-21, again in 1930-32, and again in 1942-47—the unity of the desire of all parties and sections of Indians for freedom increased steadily despite the British government propaganda about Indian disunity during those years. Also, Indian courage and self-respect increased immensely.

In granting independence, Great Britain insisted, contrary to Gandhi's advice, on splitting the country into Pakistan (predominately Moslem) and India (predominately Hindu). On this point, Congress leaders rejected Gandhi's advice. Immediately, on Moslem initiative, dreadful riots, murders and arson broke out between Moslems and Hindus. Gandhi finally quelled them. None of the violence was directed against the British. I regard the debacle as a combination of the breaking-forth of the energy of century-old frustration in subjection to foreign rule, moral fatigue of the nation at the end of the 28-year struggle for freedom, and insufficient following of Gandhi's "constructive program" which, had it been adhered to, would have cured that moral fatigue. The failure was due to not enough nonviolence.[9]

Some sociologists believe that there can be no moral progress in society because, they say, the effort involved in any moral reform is always followed by an equal reaction, a back-swing of the pendulum. Society has an inertia, they aver, that resists all substantial change.

To the extent that society is a loosely integrated organism in a low stage of development, it tends to react to a stimulus in one of the three ways described by Kotschau as mentioned above. In response to violent stimuli or to reforms introduced by coercive or deceitful methods, it presumably reacts in double phase, first yielding to the violence and then later reversing its acquiescence. But in response to honest, gentle stimuli, society is likely to act in one-phase fashion with no swing-back. Note, for example, that the social alterations caused by the stimuli of using the spade and the automobile, a tool and a machine, have been constant without, as yet, any repudiation or reverse response.

Hence the above-cited belief of certain sociologists seems to be too broad an assertion. If a reform is introduced into society by a gentle persuasion such as nonviolent resistance, the analogy indicates that the reaction would be monophasic and permanent. Considering society as an organism in a low stage of development, it may well be capable of growth into more complex integration. If so, the stimulus thereto should be nonviolent. Or society may sometimes be sick and lacking its normal balance. To restore its equilibrium and health, what is needed is a series of nonviolent stimuli.

Growth has another aspect that helps to explain the power of nonviolence. Growth results in more than increase in size. When an organism grows, there is a development of its ability to reach and use a wider range of energy. When a seed sprouts, its stem and its new leaves enable it to tap the energies of sunlight. The growing animal becomes able to roam over a considerable territory and thus enlarge its food sources, use the protection of vegetation and perhaps enlist the support of some of its own kind. The growth of a highly developed organism like man enables him to reach, mobilize, organize and use a constantly increasing range of energies and subtle forces, some in the outer world of nature, others in the intellectual and moral realms, through the cooperation and mutual assistance of his fellow men.

The wider range of energy met and used by the growing organism enables it better to maintain its equilibrium and its life in the face of adverse forces it may meet. Thus it acquires the ability to adapt itself to changes. This ability promotes survival.

Since growth takes place in response to gentle stimuli only, it would seem clear that the greater the use of gentle stimuli, the more extensive become the possibilities of growth in more and more directions, and hence the wider becomes the range of energies available to the user of gentleness.[10] In contact with this wider range of increasingly subtler forces he is either unconsciously supported by them or is consciously able to mobilize them and call upon them for support. The more he understands the method and the more he becomes aware of these subtler forces, the more he can rally them in support of a purpose that promotes their harmonious activity. By extension, that group, tribe or species which relies increasingly on gentle stimuli has the best chance for survival. That is one reason why sensitive and delicately poised man has survived the monsters of earlier ages.[11]

For these reasons the intelligent user of nonviolent resistance has for his help far greater total resources of energy and power than does his violent opponent. Some of these subtle powers are slow in action, but they are inevitably sure. History indicates that they are also more enduring than the forces of violence.

In nature, the succession of gentle stimuli creating growth heals the effects of all the violent destructive forces such as earthquakes, floods, avalanches, lightning and fires. Also, by building up forests and grasses and promoting ecologically useful wild animals, the gentle stimuli control the effects of storms and prevent floods and soil erosion. In the human realm, the stimuli of gentle kindness not only heal the effects of violence but create relationships and situations which prevent violence.

Thus the power of nonviolence and love is so similar to and so harmonious with the other subtle creative forces of nature that in the human realm it may be considered one of the higher conserving and growth-producing forces of nature. As such, it is in the long run more powerful than violence.

We have stated that one of the essential elements of successful nonviolent resistance is love, and that love is powerful. As Walt Whitman so finely said:

> "Be not dishearten'd—affection shall solve the problems of
>   Freedom yet;
> Those who love each other shall become invincible—
>   .   .   .   .   .   .

Were you looking to be held together by lawyers?
Or by an agreement on a paper? or by arms?
Nay, nor the world, nor any living thing, will so cohere."[12]

Besides the use of many repetitions of gentle stimuli, one other explanation of the power of love is this: Full-fledged love is the sentiment that grows out of awareness of the unity and wholeness of the entire human species, and expresses that awareness in all sorts of ways. As has been shown by many experiments in Gestalt psychology, the whole of anything is not only more than, but also different from, the sum of its parts.[13] Deeds informed by a loving desire for the unity and wholeness of society therefore make contact with and enlist the help not only of the forces of the separate elements of society but also of the forces that comprise and come out of its unity and wholeness. We know that sentiments—that is, organized systems of ideas and emotions—are extremely powerful in initiating, sustaining and guiding all human conduct. Of all the sentiments, love is, for the above reasons, both quantitatively and qualitatively superior. Therefore, in the long run, disciplined love always wins, and even in the short run, disciplined love wins often enough to make it far superior to violence. Furthermore, intelligent love promotes deeds which provide normal relationships, healthful surroundings and healthful and creative outlets for energy of all people of all ages. It thus reduces to a minimum frustrations, anger, resentment and violence.

In a conflict, what needs to be done is to change not people as such, but their attachment to certain ideas, sentiments, desires, and assumptions. Such changes are not effected by killing or wounding the opponents. Usually being wounded and having friends or fellow countrymen killed does not cause people to abandon their ideas, sentiments and so forth, but only to stiffen them or to postpone trying to carry them out. The growth of Communism in Russia, China and elsewhere, in spite of violent attacks on it, is a clear example of this. To get opponents to adopt new ideas, new sentiments, new assumptions, you have to get them to want the new ideas, new sentiments and new assumptions. The word "persuade" means literally "to make (something) sweet" to somebody. The new ideas must be made attractive to the opponents. Then they will take and hold the new ideas of their own will, and then the task is done. Ideas are not made attractive by harming the people whom you want to have adopt them. But love and disciplined nonviolence are persuasive.[14]

In the persuasion of nonviolent resistance, there must be not only gentleness and love but also truth. All human beings make mistakes. Adherence to truth requires public admission of our mistakes. If, out of pride or ignorance, we wait until others show up our error, then people mistrust both our ability and our honesty. But public confession of faults promotes trust because it shows: (1) a realization of one's likeness to all other people in respect to liability to error, hence a sense of human unity; (2) humility; (3) honesty; (4) disinterestedness toward one's own personal fortunes; (5) Willingness to pay the price of mistakes; hence (6) a sense of responsibility; (7) courage; (8) a revival of intelligence after a lapse into stupidity; and therefore (9) worthiness to be given another opportunity; and (10) the realization of an intellectual prerequisite to progress. When I have made a mistake in arithmetic, I cannot correct it and get the right answer until after I have admitted, at least to myself, that I made the mistake. Thus, in the moral realm, frankness and humility are modes of intelligence.

These are some of the reasons, for example, why, during World War II, after Prime Minister Churchill voluntarily admitted to Parliament that the government had made many blunders and caused grave losses and he could promise little ahead but blood and tears, Parliament immediately gave him an overwhelming vote of confidence. Unfortunately, in regard to their mistakes toward other nations, neither Churchill nor the British ruling class are as yet intelligent enough to make public admission of errors. This is true of practically all political leaders in all nations. The only exceptions I can think of are Lenin and Gandhi.

As noted in Chapter Seven, Gandhi so strongly believed in truth that he always notified his opponents in advance of what he was planning to do. At first sight, that might seem like quixotic folly. We noted there, however, that there were certain advantages in this practice. There are other advantages in thus notifying the adversary in advance of what you are planning to do. It shows a special kind of courage without threat. It is a demonstration to the opponent and the public that you are truthful even when it is risky, and that you adhere to truth and trust it even at personal sacrifice or when it does not seem at first to be to the advantage of your cause. Therefore, it suggests that you are trustworthy. It gives notice that you will not engage in deceit nor take any unfair advantage, and will not try to evade the consequences of your actions—that is, that you accept responsibility. It indicates poise and confidence in the soundness of your cause. It is a hint that you think your opponent has in him something fine and just to appeal to. Thus it is courteous. It is a suggestion that your aim is not conquest but persuasion, an appeal to moral qualities. It implies that you respect your opponent and that you have deeply pondered your past and future relationships with him. It suggests that you are aware of human unity and rely on it. All these suggestions surprise as well as tend to please the opponent and the public, and thus give you a subtle but powerful psychological advantage. We quoted in Chapter One Diderich Lund's evidence that this policy strengthened the nonviolent Norwegian resisters to the ruthless Nazis. This advantage accrues to the nonviolent resister even though he may be imprisoned as a result of forewarning his opponent.

Since trust is an essential prerequisite to persuasion, and truth creates trust, persistent devotion to truth at all costs is strongly persuasive.

Summing it up, we see that nonviolent resistance with love is able to conquer cruelty, violence, aggression, and other abuses of power because: (1) the power of many repeated gentle stimuli to cause surpassing growth of the potential decencies in the opponent is sure; (2) the user of gentle stimuli has aiding him a wider and more enduring range of forces than does the user of violence; (3) the whole is greater than the sum of its parts and since love expresses the unity and wholeness of the human species, it is a power greater than those that express only individuals or other parts of humanity; (4) intelligent love acts in advance to reduce or prevent frustrations and thereby to reduce violence to a minimum; (5) truth is an important element in nonviolence, and as truth promotes mutual trust, it is highly persuasive; and (6) these powers are effective between groups as well as between individuals.

But in a situation which is very dangerous, or where much is at stake, if someone urges me to use a new instrument, I do not adopt it when I merely learn what in general are the forces which make it work. I must also understand why and how it works in specific dangers or toward specific obstacles. I must feel sure that the risks are less than those of methods formerly used and that the estimate of probabilities is more accurate than formerly.

HERETOFORE, WE HAVE considered only broad classes of conflicts. Let us now examine in more detail certain common obstacles, namely cruelty, loss of liberty, aggression, desire to dominate, dual loyalties, hostile sentiments, the opponent's habits, paranoia or megalomania of the opponent, the opponent's assumptions, interracial conflicts, the intense discipline of certain opponents, and our own weaknesses.

Gross, persistent, intentional cruelty toward helpless people, such as the Nazi treatment of the Jews, the Japanese treatment of the Chinese during the war of 1936-1945, the British political whippings of Indians, and American lynchings and police third-degree methods, is so revolting that most decent people become indignant and can see no effective answer but counter-violence.

In Chapter Two, we discussed some of the ways by which non-violent resistance tends to reduce cruelty. But there is another kind of cruelty, which the psychologists call sadism. It is intentional. Its exercise gives the cruel person pleasure. In it there is a desire for power and an element of aggression which is the result of accumulated prior resentments created by severe repression or humiliation. The aggression is "displaced"; that is, it is not expressed toward the person who caused the original frustration but against another and weaker person. The desire for power is to make up for the sense of weakness felt at the time of the original frustration. Used against this type of cruelty, nonviolent resistance alters the desire for power, as already described, in that the reaction of the spectators teaches the cruel person that that sort of power is disadvantageous. The gentle resister proposes another channel in which the cruel person may display a more valuable kind of power. By showing respect for the personality of the cruel attacker, nonviolent resistance assuages the affront to self-respect which carried over from the original humiliations or frustrations suffered by the cruel person. These developments tend to reduce this kind of cruelty.

Another cause of cruelty is what psychologists call "projection," resulting in what is generally called making a scapegoat of someone.

Projection occurs where one is dimly aware that he has a defect of character or a wrongful motive but is unwilling to acknowledge it even to himself. This creates a conflict within him between his lower nature and his conscience. He had an underlying feeling of shame and a sense of guilt. In desperation he proceeds to "project" the fault or harmful motive upon, or impute it to, some other person or group of persons. Then he can speak of it openly, blind himself completely to its existence in himself, and attack the other person for it. Thus by this self-deception he relieves his conflict and satisfies his conscience. For his own sins the guilty person thus makes the innocent person suffer. The innocent person becomes a scapegoat.[15] In such a situation, the guilty person, by the energy of his conflict and the force of his conscience, often is fearfully cruel.

Those who for a long time have believed in the power of gentle loving-kindness will have acted accordingly, and their deeds will have had a constructive, preventive effect which will usually protect them against cruel aggression. For example, as we have observed in Chapter Six, because Quakers during and after World War I fed several million starving German children and mothers, they were less restricted or molested by the Nazis than any other religious group.

In a case of projection, nonviolent resistance alone can act but slowly. The processes described in previous chapters operate gradually to bring the attacker to true knowledge of himself. The insistence upon human unity and truth eventually overcome the divisiveness of the cruel person. But in order to secure this result the nonviolence must be free from fear or anger. In some instances, in order to provide the repetitions of stimuli mentioned above, there have to be many nonviolently resisting victims before the result is obtained. Yet, as compared with the number of victims where the reaction to the cruelty is fear, anger and violence, nonviolent resistance is less costly and more effective.

"But while we wait for this result," a skeptic might object, "the aggressor will deprive us of all our liberty and then will educate our children into his pernicious doctrines! Liberty is of supreme value. How can nonviolence preserve it?"

Liberty is not an entity which can be secured by direct effort. It is a byproduct of the creation of mutual trust and respect. Liberty is a moral affair and can be won only by moral means. After it has once been created and is threatened, true liberty cannot be preserved by violence, but only by the same moral means by which it was originally created. That wars have shifted the location of power is true, but where the result has been freedom, that freedom was, I believe, the result of other causes that were nonviolent. In the past, true freedom has been won only by mutual respect for personality, by trusting in the power of truth, and by cultivating unity, kindness and love, not merely as sentiments but by concrete, habitual deeds. Where those efforts and attitudes are found continuously, there will be freedom. Freedom has declined because we have failed to practice our ideals.

Some civil and religious liberties in the West were purchased for us by the nonviolent resistance of the first Quakers in England and by the creative, nonviolent activities of others. Many of our modern freedoms are spurious, being merely the luxurious margins allowed us by the ruling group because such allowance was the simplest way to keep the ship of state quiet and easy to handle, and because technological advances made it possible for the ruling group to grant considerable freedom to the majority without any loss of real control by the ruling group. Such freedoms are not fully moral, nor were they earned. In times of war and considerable economic decline they will decrease or depart. Some have already gone.

When our liberties are taken from us by aggressors, whether foreign or domestic, we must again earn them. We can earn them only by payment of the price, namely nonviolent resistance and the development of those conditions that create mutual trust and respect.

So it is a mistake to think that liberty is of supreme value. What is of supreme value is the origin of liberty, namely, nonviolent conduct and the above-mentioned elements which create mutual trust and mutual respect. Let those who call themselves Christians note that Christ said exceedingly little about freedom or its worth, but he laid very great stress on those attitudes and acts which result in mutual respect and trust.

Society has always regarded social order as more important even than liberty, and in times of crisis has permitted deprivation of liberties in the hope of securing order. But inasmuch as permanent order cannot be created or maintained by violence but only by the elements which create mutual respect and trust, the vigorous maintenance of those elements is more important even than order, for they are the creators not only of freedom but also of order. Christ also said very little about the importance of order.

Nor should parents be too troubled lest a cruel dictator entice or compel their children to accept his doctrines. Children who from birth have lived in an atmosphere of national frustration or resentment which has created a certain type of leader will readily accept the teachings of that leader. He expresses vocally what they subconsciously feel. But the children of a conquered nation will not accept the doctrines of a foreign conqueror. The cruelties and coercions of defeat create an energy that cannot be overcome by coercion. The history of every conquered nation is proof of that fact. Even a domestic tyrant cannot extirpate the love of liberty. It is inherent in man's very physical nervous constitution.

But we must still try to discover how the tremendous energy of aggression can be reduced by nonviolent resistance. Psychological studies indicate that a very great deal of aggression is due to earlier frustrations.[16] Every time frustration occurs in a person's life, from earliest infancy onward, the energy of the thwarted desire is dammed up inside and, unless it finds a complete and wholly satisfying substitute channel and goal, it remains bottled up as explosive energy awaiting an opportunity for release. Or we may liken the energies of frustrated desires to so many internal wound-up watch springs. We may say that there is a psychological law of conservation or persistence of the energy of emotions and of desires. People who have suffered many small frustrations or a few great ones have a great accumulation of energy seeking expression. And because of the persistence of resentment from the original frustration, this energy does not usually find release in ordinary work but prefers some form of aggression against people.

Nonviolent resistance saps this dammed-up energy by showing respect for the personality of the aggressor and thus mollifying some of the earlier resentments. Gentle resistance mobilizes and calls into action outside influences which help to change the character of the aggressor and his modes of action. Again, nonviolent resistance deprives the violent aggressor of the satisfactions which he would get from attacking a person who showed fear, anger or counter-violence. And kindness prepares the way for the acceptance by the aggressor of a proffered substitute goal and channel for his energies. It takes months or even years, but the probabilities of final success are great.

Besides frustrations, there are other causes for aggression, such as possessiveness and fear of strangers. These causes operate also among animals. Because in earlier chapters, either expressly or implicitly, we have indicated how these may be dealt with, we will not consider them further here.

But the above-mentioned factors do not always offset all the energy of aggression. The absorption of the surplus energy of aggression rests on a different set of considerations.

In relation to all other species of living organisms, the human species is a unit. Its elements are individual persons and they have among themselves certain differences and certain similarities. However important the differences may seem, the similarities and unities are deeper, more enduring and more important. This is true also as between various groups, such as civilizations, races, nations, tribes, religious groups, socio-economic systems and social classes. The unities and the interworking of differences are such that the human species as a whole may for some purposes be considered a loosely integrated organism. If that be true, then, as in any organism, an injury to one part harms all the other parts, injures their harmonious working and upsets their equilibrium. Each part suffers and endures the suffering. If the original injury is an infection, some of the neighboring parts, which are, so to say, wholly innocent, may even die from the injury. In a healthy organism the parts thus indirectly injured do not strike back but, as it were, offer their energies for a curative process. Their energy absorbs the shock to the whole organism. Thus the equilibrium of the whole organism is gradually restored.

When by aggression the moral equilibrium of society has been upset, in order to restore that equilibrium and regain moral health, part of the energy of the aggression must be cushioned and absorbed by the nonviolent voluntary suffering of persons who may be wholly innocent of the frustrations that caused the aggression, and relatively innocent of possessiveness or fear of strangers.

The innocent have always suffered for the sins of the guilty. If each of us reaped only what he individually had sown, no more and no less, it would be unjust for the innocent to suffer for the guilty. But in this world, each person does not reap, either of good or evil, just what he has sown. Each of us enjoys a share of the entire tech-

nical, intellectual, and moral advances that have accumulated in society since the dawn of human history. This is vastly more than any
of us could make by himself or deserves or has earned. In the same
way, each of us carries part of the load of mistakes and wrongs committed by our forefathers and our contemporaries, irrespective of biological inheritance or apparent national or racial community. Furthermore, very few are wholly innocent. Most of us condone or support
evil institutions or public wrongs of many sorts. Most of us have, in
some degree, pride, selfishness and desire for power over others. The
guilty suffer, too, though often unawares. That is, their losses may
be subtler, more indirect and slower to arrive, but they are deeper
and injure not so much their bodies as their minds and souls.

Regarding both innocent and guilty as parts of a great organism, the innocent necessarily must suffer. Indeed, their suffering is
proof of the organic unity of humanity. If they did not suffer, it
would mean that they had no connection with the rest of the species.
Their suffering is proof that the differences between all persons are
not so important as the unities and similarities.

In this aspect of the matter, the difference between guilt and in-
nocence is relatively superficial. The common life, the life of the
species, is more important, and the prime duty of the innocent is not
toward securing justice but toward restoring the moral health and
equilibrium of the entire human society all over the world. I do not
mean that those who suffer injustice should timidly lie down under
it, but that the aim of their nonviolent resistance should be more
than justice. They cannot restore the equilibrium of society by counter-violence but only by resolute patience, forgiveness, love, kindly
nonviolent resistance and voluntary suffering. Happily, the very use
of these nonviolent means will bring not only justice for themselves but moral balance for society. Though they may not have
asked for it, the relatively innocent have the tough but surpassingly
important task of saving humanity.

In a moral realm such as the world of mankind, mistakes and
wrongs must necessarily be paid for and corrected. Because the
world is complex and constantly changing and some people's lives are
short, the payments and corrections are not usually fully made by
those who make the mistakes. Whenever someone causes a frustration, it is paid for in part by other persons.

But happily, because this is a moral world, if payment for wrong is voluntarily undertaken by anyone, and nonviolent suffering for it is assumed with love, the full payment does not have to be made. It is, as it were, discounted.

Justice alone would require full payment of every moral debt. Justice deals with the mutual relations of the elements of society. So does love. But love, as previously explained, is more powerful because it also expresses the forces of the whole. Thus, as compared with justice, love brings more forces into the healing process and re-establishes the moral equilibrium more rapidly and easily. Without need for balancing off every separate wrong by an equal separate right, love instead balances off part of the wrongs by the forces of the whole. Therefore, loving action, such as voluntary suffering with love for the sake of principle, is never dissipated or lost. Sooner or later it bears fruit. Gentle loving-kindness thus absorbs and counterbalances the extra energy of aggression. By comparison with a struggle of mutual violence, nonviolent resistance enables the forces of the whole to reduce greatly the destruction, losses and sufferings.

If we had to rely on justice alone to right the sum total of all the mistakes and evils inherited from the past, as well as those of the present, the situation would seem well-nigh hopeless. But nonviolence and love can change our despair to hope.

In most conflicts, there is present in both parties the desire to dominate. We may say that the prevailing concept of human relationships involves dominance of one person and subordination of the other.[17] This assumption prevails in the family as between parents and children and as between the older and younger children, in school as between teacher and pupils, and in industry and agriculture as between employer and employee. War is merely an application of this same pattern in a critical situation between nations. People accept wars because they do not see the possibility of any other pattern of human relationships.

But nonviolent resistance, together with kindness, offers an entirely different pattern based on a relationship not of dominance-submission but of integration. This is a relationship that often exists momentarily and could be made permanent and prevalent. This relationship is not a denial of differences of qualities and function; it does not abolish division of labor or differences of function. In this relationship, each party is in search of common purposes in activities that are mutually satisfying to himself and others. Each party is sure of his essential nature, shows trust and expects trust. Each is eager for growth and aware that growth means change in himself and his relationships, and is respectful of the personality of others, free from fear, and eager for truth. Under such circumstances, each person will spontaneously yield when by so doing he can promote the common purpose or win closer to the truth. To promote this, he will sacrifice himself for truth and for the search for common purpose. He is willing to have his actions and his vision tested by the actions, ideas and values of other persons. The result of such interaction is not compromise but growth and adaptation, a change of character without loss of personal integrity.[18] If there is a loss or injury of possessions, there is an increase in security. If there is a change in social status, it is an improvement and it is realized as such by the person undergoing it.

But it is no wonder that violent persons assume at first that nonviolent resistance is merely crazy and that nonviolent resisters are as eager as anyone else for dominance. The long history and wide prevalence of the pattern of dominance-submission blinds the violent person to the possibility of any other sort of human relationship, to say nothing of his possible ability to help create such a different relationship. He feels that if he yields even a trifle, his opponent will take advantage of him and try to dominate him and harm his security, social status and personal integrity. Knowing also the energy of resentment against frustrations, and more or less aware that his dominance causes frustrations in other people, he feels the need of being constantly on guard and has a sense of constant uncertainty and insecurity. The source of all attempts at dominance is this deep sense of insecurity. To reduce the desire for dominance, this sense of insecurity must be relieved.

There are several elements in nonviolent resistance which tend to reduce in the violent opponent this feeling of insecurity. Some of them are respect for personality, good will, acts of kindness, adherence to truth, disciplined order, a belief that human unity and underlying similarities are more enduring and important than human differences, and a steady series of deeds in accord with that belief. Another important factor in relieving the violent person's sense of insecurity is the nonviolent resister's faithfulness to his method despite losses of property, physical injury, imprisonment, or even death. Such proofs of sincerity are highly persuasive. If in time of crisis the advocate of nonviolence abandons that method and in alleged necessary self-defense resorts to violence, the onlookers and the violent opponent say, "Aha! He talked pretty smoothly, but in a pinch he believes that you must dominate or be dominated. His talk of a new system of human relationships is hypocritical bunk."

Where the nonviolent resister is killed in the struggle, his sincerity and devotion raise up others to support his cause. This is proved by many instances, chief of which is the continuance and spread of Christianity despite the violent death of its founder and the persecutions of his followers for centuries. Admitting all the failures of the churches, there are still enough real followers of Christ to make this statement true. The vitality of nonviolent resistance enables its trust-promoting qualities to endure and the repetition of stimuli to be prolonged. Even in the extreme case, and indeed because of the extreme case, the sense of insecurity in the violent party is relieved. Then dominance seems less necessary and the first steps of creating the new set of relationships can be begun. When that new framework can be gradually institutionalized, the desire for dominance, except in abnormal persons, will be gone.

The dominance of some people is often called forth by an unwillingness in many to accept and exercise responsibility, and by a desire of others to be dominated. Certain people, perhaps because of lack of energy, prefer to acquire self-respect and give dignity to their ego not by their own exertions but by some mode of subordinate association or identification, often only fanciful, with those whom they consider great or with a big corporation or a powerful government. Some subordination grows out of political or economic ignorance.

In all these instances, the dominance of the rulers is a result of the weakness of the masses. Nonviolent resistance and its discipline tends to remove such weaknesses among those who practice it, and thus tends to weaken the dominance of those in power.

In regard to the desire to dominate, I would distinguish the instances where the violently dominating person or group has a bona fide ability for management and administration. There certainly are such people, born with a keen ability to understand human relationships and a capacity for organizing and stimulating people to joint endeavors. Such a talent is of much social value, provided it is exercised without pride, selfishness or coercion, and in a sincere and pure spirit of service. It would be a grave mistake to completely deprive such people of an opportunity to function just because many of them have warped the situation to their own advantage and have used violence. I would therefore be quite willing to allow such talented people to stand for office and be chosen by democratic process to act as government executives, provided they are subject to the veto power of well-trained nonviolent resistance by those whose affairs they may administer.

To such persons the nonviolent resisters could wisely say, in effect, "We do not seek to deprive you of your true status and function, but merely to get you to purge yourself of the desire to dominate and coerce us. If you will truly serve the people unselfishly and honestly and without coercion, we will be glad to have you exercise your undoubted talents." When once that understanding got home, the energy of skilled administrators who also are sincere would in many cases leave the road of selfishness and violence and seek a satisfactory settlement. Their essential social status being made secure, they would perhaps be more willing to yield up their former privileges and adapt themselves to a new situation.

The combination of this pattern of dominance-submission and the relation between frustration and aggression makes it clear why violence does not solve conflicts. It may change their form but it does not end them. Violence ends in the frustration of the defeated party. Because the energy of emotion, intellect, and will is persistent, frustration inevitably creates some sort of subsequent aggression, perhaps against someone else. That causes another outburst of violence, ending in another frustration, and so to endless waste, cruelty, suffering and loss. The vicious circle can be broken only by indomitable patience, nonviolent resistance and kindness. The price is high, but very much less than that of violence.

Often another obstacle for nonviolent resistance to overcome is what may be called the opponent's dual loyalty—his loyalty to standards of personal morality and his loyalty to his group, whether that group be a society, a corporation, a social class, a government, a nation or an unorganized race. Often these two loyalties clash because of a conflict between the moral codes and purposes of the private person and the moral codes and purposes of the group.[19] This conflict may be severe enough almost to constitute a kind of schizophrenia. It is probably one of the causative factors in the enormous amount of mental disease in the modern world.

Out of a sense of duty to the nation, a man who in private life has the highest standards of rectitude will, in his capacity as a government official or diplomat, publicly and emphatically tell a lie. There was a famous example of this during World War I when Sir Edward Grey, then foreign minister for Great Britain, in a speech to Parliament denied the existence of the secret treaties with Russia and France which he himself had taken part in making and which were revealed to the world later when the Bolsheviks seized power in Russia. Similar instances occur in the political life of the United States and most other nations. In the same way, many officers of large industrial corporations in controversies with labor unions will, out of loyalty to what they believe to be the interests of the corporation, engage in deceit and violence which would be utterly foreign to them in their personal relationships.

Because of this dual loyalty, nonviolent resisters to such an organization's policies will find men of fine personal character as the leaders of their opponents ordering or acquiescing in acts of atrocious injustice, seemingly adamant against appeals to human decency.

Continued nonviolent resistance overcomes this difficulty in two ways. It gradually clarifies the relation between means and ends. It leads opponents who have come to think of the existence and habitual functioning of their organization as so important that it is an end in itself, to realize that their organization originally was and still is only a means to a finer and greater end. That realization may lead them to see that the organization, or its accustomed modes of action, can be altered so as to accomplish better the finer end. Again, nonviolent resistance, in ways that are not yet clear, not only solves cases of opposition and conflict between two persons, or two groups, but also integrates the different levels or compartments into which men divide their lives. This process takes place in both the nonviolent resister and his violent opponent. If the violent opponent, out of loyalty to his organization, is doing acts inconsistent with personal morality, the gradual increase of integration within him will enable him somehow to resolve that inconsistency and bring the organization's moral code more closely in line with personal morality.

Sentiments play a great part in the affairs of all people. From all the discussions in previous chapters it is not difficult to see that nonviolent resistance plus friendliness can alter the sentiments which control the opponent. Some sociologists think that sentiments change so exceedingly slowly that for any person to make persistent attempts to change the sentiments of others is a mark of immaturity or stupidity. Yet who would deny that Buddha, Plato, Jesus Christ, Mohammed, Martin Luther, Galileo, Newton, Marx, Lenin, Gandhi, Sun Yat-sen and Mao Tse-tung altered the sentiments of millions? And who would accuse these men of immaturity? The last forty years have seen a great development of the sentiment of nationality among the hundreds of millions of China and India. Sentiments can be altered, and modern psychology has indicated some of the ways.

The reluctance of people to change their habits of thought, feeling and action is a form of inertia which comprises another obstacle for nonviolent resistance to overcome. The longer the habit is continued, the harder it is to change.

Part of the strength of habit lies in the fact that in habit there is an element of pattern, partly of intellect and imagination, partly of sentiment, partly of will and action. One of the greatest aids to change of habit is, then, a change of intellectual pattern. By its stimulus to the imagination of the opponent, nonviolent resistance causes such a change of pattern and thus brings about the desired change of habit. The greater significance and moral beauty in the pattern of nonviolent resistance aid its ability to alter other habits.

In some instances, the nonviolent resister may have to struggle against a person or group of persons afflicted with real megalomania or even paranoia. In such cases, the only successful treatment by psychiatry has been by means of steady friendliness and nonviolence, working from an area of clear perception in the patient to a clear understanding of his error and a better knowledge of himself. Nonviolent resistance is a sort of "field psychiatry." It takes time and involves suffering by the nonviolent party. But the method is effective and creative, and it is the only method that is effective.[20]

Since the assumptions of people in conflict are usually different, and also control conduct, probably no conflict can be permanently solved unless the pertinent assumptions of one or both parties are changed. This may or may not require recognition, explicit formulation and acknowledgement of the assumptions, but it is an important part of persuasion. Changing an opponent's assumptions is a step toward causing him to experience a deep-going change of heart, for a person's assumptions lie very deep. Assumptions exist prior to any reasoning. They cannot be either proved or disproved by logic. They precede explicit beliefs. Like axioms in geometry or rules in a game, they are at the basis of all of a person's actions and govern their character and direction. A person may occasionally be dimly aware of his assumptions, but more often he is wholly unconscious of them, some assumptions are relative, depending on still deeper assumptions; others are absolute.

The search for one's assumptions, whether made by oneself or someone else, requires keen discrimination, honesty, disinterestedness, and close thinking. It is disquieting. The more nearly absolute the assumption, the more one resists the search. Dragging up roots is painful. To have to face one's own assumptions in the clear light of full consciousness brings out so many unforeseen implications that the sudden revelation is often startling. Sometimes inconsistencies appear that are most uncomfortable. The sudden demand for thinking out all the implications, interconnections and inconsistencies of one's assumptions calls for more time and energy than one is willing to devote. It is felt as a strain. It may even involve humiliation.

Since assumptions lie so deep, it is hard to see how they can be changed. One thing that makes it possible to effect change in them is the fact that assumptions do not exist singly and separately either in a person or in a civilization. Assumptions exist, as it were, in constellations in which some are dominant and others recessive. The elements are not entirely consistent or harmonious. The constellations are therefore not in perfect equilibrium but are in a more or less unstable state of strain or tension.

Nonviolent resistance is a deep, thorough and persistent search for truth. It operates both in the conscious mind and also in the imagination and subconscious. It permeates all areas of the lives of both opponents. This search therefore tests assumptions, and if some of them are mistaken, the strain upon them is increased. Presently, because of the unstable equilibrium plus the new strain, the constellation has to alter, and with this comes an alteration in the mistaken assumption. The process takes time, but in persuasion such alterations are of great importance.

There is probably one other way in which assumptions are altered. When remarkable results are obtained by a new method, people are compelled to re-examine all the thinking that went into their previous methods, and sometimes to carry their analysis clear back to the assumptions that underlie the methods and revise them. The careful and precise use of the inductive method of logic in science during the past few centuries has produced such notable results that thinkers all over the western world have had to change many of their former assumptions. So, after considerable victories have been won by nonviolent resistance, those who have lost those struggles will be likely to modify their prior assumptions.

Lack of space prevents more detailed discussion of the manner of such changes. But it will be useful to enumerate here some typical mistaken assumptions which the nonviolent resister will likely encounter. Most of them are relative, but some are absolute:

1. That the only practical human relationship is of dominance on one side and submission on the other.

2. That other people are a means for the purposes of those who dominate.

3. That because social order is of primary importance, the particular social order now existent is the only valuable and practical social orders and therefore must be rigidly maintained. This assumption is often made also as to the existing political system.

4. That a valued end justifies the use of any means.

5. That management or ruling is the most important of all social functions.

6. That therefore managers and rulers should be rewarded by extra privileges and greater wealth of all kinds.

7. That those now in control necessarily have superior fitness to govern (or that they are necessarily unfit).

8. That those now in control are in all ways superior people (or that they are in all ways inferior).

9. That those who are physically strong, those who control the most technical knowledge, the most machines, the most materials, or the largest markets, are the ones who do survive and that only they should survive.

10. That managers or rulers are not subject to the poison of power, nor to corruption, and are not as selfish as others—and that there are no degrees and gradations in government or management.

11. That practically all other people are predominantly selfish, greedy, envious, and desirous of superior power.

12. That the weaknesses of mankind are greater than their virtues.

13. That money is the most important value.

14. That the possession of money is a sign and proof of political and social worth.

15. That production of material goods is more important than the production of healthy and normal people and of sound human relationships, or that the former automatically produces the latter.

16. That certain races, nations or classes are incapable of self-government and should not be allowed even a veto power over what they are told to do.

17. That in an organization, great size is proof of its value to society.

18. That institutions are more important than people. (Note here that society is not an institution.)

19. That there is no supreme unifying principle or axiom more inclusive and more fundamental than the principle which scientists assume underlies and unites all natural forces. (Cf. Collingwood, above cited.)

20. That if there is a supreme unifying principle, it is not really and constantly as powerful in men's affairs as, for instance, the force of gravitation.

21. That this supreme unifying principle is not immanent in all people but, if at all, only in certain select individuals including the rulers, or in certain select nations. (Such immanence would be somewhat like the immanence of the axioms in all geometrical propositions, or of the rules of a chess game in the players and the pieces used.)

Interracial antagonisms are another obstacle which nonviolent resistance will meet. They are complex. In part they are economic or "class" phenomena, in part political, in part social. They involve all of the obstacles already discussed: mistaken assumptions, fear of strangers, pride, possessiveness, cruelty, desire to dominate, frustration and aggression, habit and dual loyalty. This very complexity however, serves to emphasize the utter futility and stupidity of using violence as a solution. That method can produce nothing but more violence and ultimately destruction of all the different civilizations and their total freight of human values. While the complexity indicates that the solutions will require great patience and forbearance and will necessarily be slow, nevertheless the only means of solution are love and nonviolent resistance.

There is not space here to discuss every possible kind of opposition that may be met in an opponent to nonviolence. But those we have discussed are perhaps the main types. There are in nonviolence more elements of strength than we yet know. The discussion will perhaps serve to reassure the doubters of the persuasive power of nonviolence and thus lead them to try it.

But there is yet another kind of obstacle which nonviolent resisters will meet and must overcome. It resides not in their opponents but in themselves. It is made up of the inconsistencies, weaknesses, temptations and corruptions that beset nonviolent resisters, as well as their attachment to certain habits and institutions that are inconsistent with nonviolence. These resisters are all common human clay and subject to defects. The overcoming of these defects is part of the function of training and discipline and will be discussed in the following chapters.

Lastly, we should realize that we must learn how to persuade not only our active opponents but also those who are indifferent, those who are curious spectators, and our children and ourselves. For all these kinds of persuasion, we need a thorough understanding of the method of nonviolence, its working and its disciplines. We must know what are the methods and disciplines and how and why they work.

10

THE NEED FOR TRAINING

For various reasons, many people see no necessity for training for nonviolent resistance. Many are even repelled by the idea. Some think that such training would produce unpleasant self-consciousness or even insincerity and smug self-righteousness. Others think it is liable to lead to dogmatism and fanaticism. Some see it resulting in loss of initiative, dreary uniformity or boredom. These various objections will be dealt with in the following discussion.

While any course of action or inaction, if unwisely pursued, has dangers, that is no reason for holding off from useful action. Let us consider some reasons why training for action is useful.

The general environment and herd pressure are powerful, constant influences upon every one of us. They will assuredly bend and mold us into the prevailing pattern unless we take specific measures and make special efforts to do otherwise. Nonviolent resistance is different from the usual course of conduct and different from our primitive reactions. It will therefore require efforts specially designed. Regular training is a specially designed and specially potent factor of one's environment. Since peacetime military conscription has apparently become permanent in the United States, most of us (or our children)—unless we are over-age, unfit or conscientious objectors assigned to alternative service—will be disciplined into the military mold and compelled to fight.

All of us are creatures of habit. Habits are necessary in order to save energy and enable us to use our minds. If I had to direct consciously every muscle in my legs to act in right tension and right sequence all the time I was walking, I would hardly have time enough even to steer in a certain direction, to say nothing of planning what to do when I got to my destination. If I am active, I have one kind of habits, if lazy I have another kind. Always I have some sort of habits. Hence I must choose which kind of habits I want to have; and, having chosen, I must then subject myself to the process of learning, of habit formation, that will produce that particular kind of habitual action. To be effective, nonviolent resistance must be habitual. To establish such a new habit calls for a somewhat prolonged process of habit formation.

One name for this process of habit formation is discipline.

We have seen that growth of all kinds requires many repetitions of slight stimuli. This is another way of describing one important aspect of the learning process, that is to say, of training.

In the modern world our moral relationships are often complex and confusing. For this reason, very few people can instantly think, in many events involving conflict, just what is the right thing to do. Therefore, previous training in an effective way of solving conflicts would be a great help. As Gerald Heard has pointed out, at the instant when action is demanded of us, we do not have time to think through the whole situation, and so we act according to our assumptions, our sentiments and our habits. Hence, if we prefer a certain kind of action, it is wise to prepare in advance the sentiments and habits that will automatically produce that kind of action.

At this point, let us consider the alleged dangers of training for nonviolent resistance. Take the fear that it would lead to priggishness or insincerity. Can that fear be based on the idea that learning an effective method of handling conflicts is morally dangerous to those who use it?

Resort to the courts is one mode of handling conflicts, but nobody hesitates to study law because it might make him priggish or insincere. Personal violence is another mode of dealing with conflict, but nobody refrains from learning to box or wrestle or to shoot for fear of becoming smug. War is yet another method of handling large-scale conflict, but nobody dreads the study of military science lest it make him self-righteous. Nonviolent resistance endeavors to influence other people intellectually and morally, but so also do politics and the arts and sciences of child care, education, and psychiatry. Nobody considers those studies likely to make a person morally unpleasant.

Let nobody think that acquiring skill in nonviolent resistance results in superficial actions which do not grow naturally and truly out of an inner condition, hence resulting in hypocrisy. The changes induced by the training, just as in military training, alter the source of the responses as well as the responses themselves. Of course, if one does not understand the need for training and the reasons for and results of each detail in the training, it may become a meaningless ritual, and one then may become insincere. But that can happen in any discipline—scientific, religious, esthetic or military—and is not due to the discipline itself.

Again, let nobody think that acquiring skill in nonviolent resistance means becoming saintly. Formerly, nonviolence was practiced only by saints, but it is no longer so limited. The invention of a discipline has changed that. A discipline is like a tool. Tools, whether tangible or intangible, make it possible for ordinary men to do what formerly was possible only to men of very unusual skill, strength or intellect. The mold-board plow, for example, makes it possible for every farmer to cultivate even more land than only a very skilled and powerful man could formerly do. A thousand years ago, very few people could read or do geometrical problems. The invention of printing, plus institutionalized public education, made it possible for practically everyone both to read and to develop skill in geometry. Military discipline, another kind of tool, changes men of indifferent courage into heroes. So Gandhi's invention of a discipline for nonviolent resisters made this method possible for hundreds of thousands of Indian peasants who were not saints but ordinary people. Hence, if a person now decides to undergo training for nonviolence, he is not priggishly announcing that he is going to be a saint, nor should anyone attribute to him that intention or attitude.

A person does not create moral power. It comes to him only after he has complied with certain principles. This compliance enables him to tap the spiritual power pervading the entire world, just as one by suitable connections and switches can tap an electric current from a power circuit. Spiritual power then manifests itself in that person in the mode of moral power. The moral power is created by the spiritual power, not by the person who makes the contact, just as electric light is created not by the bulb but by the current that flows through it. So if a person becomes proud of having moral power, his understanding of the situation is badly mistaken. If a person were to get smug over training to become nonviolent, he would be so mistaken about the whole matter that under provocation he would probably fail and become violent.

Nonviolent resistance is a more intelligent mode of conduct than violence, but to become proud of learning to be more intelligent in human relationships betrays immaturity and is itself unintelligent. If, despite these considerations, some persons get priggish or proud because they are learning or have learned to use nonviolent resistance habitually, it means not that the training for such skill is at fault, but probably that they themselves have a tendency to that personal weakness.

It is true that a certain type of training might cause dogmatism or fanaticism. But that would not be peculiar to nonviolence; it could happen in training for law, theology, medicine, engineering or warfare. Hence the objection can be postponed until you see or experience the discipline itself. The same considerations apply to three other alleged dangers—unpleasant uniformity, reduction of initiative, and boredom.

Some may think that discipline and its resultant habits are incompatible with freedom. That is not so. The original decision to undergo discipline must be voluntary and without coercion. But without self-discipline and good habits, nobody can have a sound character or achieve anything worthwhile. Even the wind, the very symbol of complete freedom, is at all times subject to the limitations and laws of aerodynamics, of thermodynamics, of gravity, and other physical laws. There can be no human freedom without strict and habitual adherence to moral and intellectual principles.

We have maintained that nonviolent resistance is a persuasive assertion of the unity of the human species, and that this unity is more important, stronger, deeper and more enduring than any differences of race, custom, culture, ideas, social or financial status, education or economic-political systems. Yet again and again such differences seem to be more powerful and persistent, so it is sometimes very difficult to believe that intangible human unity (some would call it spirit) is still more powerful. The hesitation of most people to trust in the power of that unity is quite understandable.

It is a little like learning how to swim. Before I learned how to swim, I did not realize that the water displaced by floating objects acts as an upthrusting force upon the floating object. I was well aware of the weight of my body, but had never compared it with the weight of an equivalent body of water. I did not know that when my lungs are filled with air, the total weight of my body becomes slightly less than an equivalent weight of water—just enough to enable the upthrust of the displaced water to make me float in the water barely above the surface, and, in proper position, enable me to breathe. I had of course seen corks, logs, boats and bits of wood floating safely on top of the water, and had been in boats so floating. I had breathed all my life. I had seen other people swim. But to combine the familiar breathing with unfamiliar posture and movements and a force that I had never before explicitly recognized as applicable to my own body—that was frightening. To trust my own body and life to this new and only faintly recognized force of buoyancy, to sink into the water until I felt it come into my ears, eyes, nose and mouth so that I could not breathe—that was terrifying. To trust this force, to try these new positions and motions, was contrary to all my instincts.

But other people who were my own age, and not in other respects more gifted than I, were doing it around me and offered to help. So I regained enough faith and self-confidence to try again. I wanted that power and skill and the fun I saw come from it. I wanted to be more of a person than I was. Many times I choked and got water in my lungs. But each time I also became more aware of the buoyant power of the water, and gradually I learned the new postures and movements that enabled me to use it. Finally, I, like the others, learned how to keep my nose and eyes above water. Then with practice I developed skill and self-confidence. Now, even if the water beneath me is a mile deep, I can swim safely on top. The margin of safety seems narrow, but it is sufficient. Despite the risks, swimming is a method of attaining safety in the water that is vastly more effective than the instinctive struggles of the person who does not know how to swim. On such narrow margins, with such delicate balances and integrations, life of all kinds has proceeded all down the ages. So the subtle, intangible power of the spirit of human unity is to be trusted. It can be secured by learning the right ways of believing and making them into habits.[1]

Men do not learn to improve their relationships by studying history. They make an advance only when experience, thought and imagination have eventually crystallized in the invention of a tool. The tool may be material, like a plow, or immaterial, like a concept, a symbol or an alphabet. A material tool acts on the environment; an immaterial tool acts on man's own inner thought or character and thus helps control his behavior. The regular use of such a tool creates an advance without any further effort especially aimed at such improvement.

The discipline for nonviolence is, then, like military discipline, an intangible tool. It makes the idea effective. Steady use of this tool will make a vast improvement in human relationships.

In order to bring up children into the way of nonviolence, there must be provided a special mode of family life and training during their formative years. This must be such as will reduce frustrations to a minimum and provide prompt and satisfying outlets for the energy of such frustrations.[2] The child must always have an environment of steady affection and firm guidance.

Without discipline, that is to say, without a mode of habit formation and maintenance, neither a group nor an idea can win power. And without a great increase in group power or idea power you cannot attain or keep for long any social, political or economic reforms. Mere education or organization will not permanently secure any reforms.

Reforms will come to stay only if the masses acquire and retain the ability to make a firm veto by mass nonviolent resistance. This holds true for such proposals as the single tax, socialism, money reforms, better education, abolition of war, decentralization, cooperatives, abolition of interracial discrimination, industrial democracy or whatever other reform you may desire. Hence reformers would be wise to lay less stress upon advocacy of their special changes and concentrate on the teaching of nonviolent resistance. Once that tool is mastered, we can make all sorts of permanent reforms.

Sooner or later, some nonviolent resisters will find themselves condemned to prison. To endure imprisonment successfully, and all the cruelty that goes with it, they will need firm discipline.

If a person wants to do anything that is socially valuable—for instance, to become a physician, a farmer, a dietician or a mechanic—he cheerfully undergoes several years of training, during which he learns a specific skill and in that respect learns to think more exactly than other people. If he really cares for his occupation, he keeps on training himself all the rest of his life. In that way he succeeds. The moral is obvious for believers in nonviolence.

Unless each one of us becomes more self-controlled and skilled in human relationships, is it not vain to hope for a better world? Does each one of us expect to stay just as he is and have all the self-improvement made by other people? Is all the wrong somebody else's fault? Should everybody blame somebody else? Should everybody "pass the buck"? If we believers in nonviolence refused to change our habits in thorough fashion—that is, refused to undergo discipline—the refusal would imply that in any conflict in which we became involved, we thought the opponent was entirely in the wrong and was the only one who must change. Since we all make mistakes and do wrong things, the wrongs are never entirely on the part of the oponent. But even if, in any particular conflict, all the changing must be done by the opponent, to anounce such an assumption in advance would not be persuasive. A "holier than thou" attitude is always iritating and bad tactics. We who believe in nonviolence must change our habits before we ask an opponent to change his.

Again, if we believers in nonviolence decline to change our habits, the refusal indicates that we think we can win any struggle very easily. That is a silly miscalculation. He who makes it will practically always be defeated.

Before a person can influence or change another person, he must, unless a born genius, first change himself. This, of course, is true also among groups. Marxians profess to believe that the only important formative human influence is that of institutions, and that our efforts must be devoted entirely to changing our institutions. But the Communists in Russia took good care to kill the Tsar, and the Stalinists "purged" and executed numerous former party leaders and drove Trotsky clear to Mexico and finally killed him there. By so doing these prominent Marxians thereby tacitly admitted the primary influential power of disciplined individual persons. Institutions are group habits of persons. Before there can be institutions there must be individual persons. A change of character or of abilities can be secured only by training and change of habits. Newton influenced other men of science only after he had, by hard work, altered his own concepts of the mechanics of the solar system. Lenin influenced other people only after a long period of thinking and self-discipline. That is true of every influential person in all history, and of every influential organization. Hence nonviolent resisters in order to alter opponents must first subject themselves to self-discipline.

The practical effectiveness of pacifism may justifiably be doubted until the movement as a whole adopts and practices an adequate discipline.

Unless he practices such a discipline, a person who has nonviolence as one of his ideals will, if his country is attacked, usually end by supporting the war. At the outbreak of World War II, this happened to many highly intelligent pacifists, among them Einstein, Bertrand Russell and A. A. Milne. The reasons for this may be that (a) without considerable discipline, his assumptions, sentiments, and habits of thought will not have changed enough to keep him steady, and so he succumbs to the herd pressure; or (b) he fails to realize that order and liberty are not entities in their own right but are byproducts of deeper conditions; or (c) he really values certain institutions, his property or his own social status, more than the human lives that are forfeited in war.

Since the innocent common people always suffer for the mistakes and greeds of their rulers, political or economic, it is up to the innocent to control their rulers. In our increasingly centralized society, public affairs are so complex, the scale of political organization is so great, and daily work is so absorbing and pressing that the common man has no time to examine all proposals, make decisions and lead in public affairs. He must delegate all that to specialists. And because of the inevitable poison of power, such delegates often become selfish or corrupt. Propaganda is so pervasive and bewildering, and the machinery of voting and representation so complex and warped, that real control by the people in matters of ultimate power is nearly impossible with that machinery. The only power left to the people is the power of veto, and in ultimate matters that can be exercised effectively only by mass nonviolent resistance. Hence the people must thoroughly learn this method.

11

TRAINING

W E NEED SOMETHING for workers for peace that would be equivalent to the Army Field Service Manual that is issued for instruction to all soldiers. This chapter is intended for that purpose. It is only a beginning, but when we get into the doing of these first steps we will come to see more clearly further modes of discipline and further kinds of action.

TAKE A LEAF OUT OF THE SOLDIER'S BOOK

IF CONSTRUCTIVE pacifists are to be engaged in action that is a substitute for war, and that must be made just as effective as war, let us try to learn from military men. They know so well how to prepare for vigorous, effective, prolonged action.

Before men become soldiers, they have a general idea of the purpose and methods of war. Military authorities, in training men, develop in them a much clearer detailed idea of the purpose and methods of war, and along with that certain strong sentiments.* Then they require frequent, regular, prolonged practice in doing many of the things which will have to be done in war, especially practice in shooting at targets.[1] The wisdom and effectiveness of these methods have been proven through the long history of warfare. They were made especially clear during the two world wars.

Human action in varying situations is most effective when the person acting understands the meaning and purpose of his acts, can relate them to a larger pattern of conduct of human purpose, which he values and accepts, has a clear sense of the direction and orienta-

---

* In this chapter, I use the term "sentiment" as meaning a systematized habit of feeling and an integrated system of ideas and emotions.

tion of his purpose and life, and has no inner conflict or inconsistencies of desire in relation to his action.[2] Our sentiments determine and control our emotions and much of our conduct.[3] The immense power of the sentiment of patriotism is a good example. Another example is your emotional reaction if you are suddenly knocked down by a man without warning. If that happens to you on the street, you get angry. If it happens while you are engaged in a football game, you don't get angry. The difference between your emotional reactions in these two cases is caused entirely by the difference in your sentiments or state of mind at those times. Since you can cultivate a sentiment until it becomes habitual, it is clear that by taking time you can control at least the character of your emotions and actions.

Let us then follow the analogy of military training, realizing that while our purposes and methods are different from those of the soldier, we are aiming at a substitute for violence and war and can therefore use some of the knowledge of human character which soldiers have learned.

SPECIAL SITUATION REQUIRES SPECIAL CARE

FIRST, IN REGARD TO understanding the general purposes and methods of settling conflicts, the soldier with this method is at an advantage, because even before he was a soldier he knew, as all civilians know, a good deal about warfare. The man who has decided to use the nonviolent method of persuasion is undertaking a new line of conduct. It is likely that he has not been familiar with it from his childhood, as is the case with the soldier. Hence he will have to make an intensive and careful study of his method and its advantages as compared with the method of violence and war. Constructive resisters must therefore read or listen to their leaders and discuss their method until they understand it thoroughly.

Until we get a considerable number of people to understand thoroughly the method and how to practice it, the leaders, at least, will have to rely much on books and pamphlets. It is not necessary always for the rank and file to read about the subject, as was shown by the instances of partly or wholly successful nonviolent resistance in Norway, South Africa and Montgomery, Alabama. But the leaders must understand it and the rank and file must trust the leaders and learn from them what to do and not do. The more reading on the subject can be done by all the participants, the better the chances of success. After a considerable number have mastered the method, probably most of the training can be done by word of mouth and by example, as is the case in military discipline.

GET YOUR BEARINGS

I STRONGLY RECOMMEND that each believer in nonviolence intending to train, especially the leaders, read the following:

The Autobiography of Mohandas K. Gandhi (Boston: Beacon Press, 1957);

Louis Fischer, *The Life of Mahatma Gandhi* (New York: Mentor 1954);

Henry David Thoreau, "Civil Disobedience," in *Walden and Other Writings* (New York: Modern Library 1950);

Martin Luther King, *Stride toward Freedom* (New York: Harper 1959); and if you can afford the price,

Joan V. Bondurant, *Conquest of Violence* (Princeton, N. J.: Princeton University Press 1959).

There are of course hundreds of books on the different aspects of peace and war and social conflicts and their causes, but selection is necessary. I think the above five, more than any others, have in them the facts and ideas which will be most useful to believers in nonviolent resistance to injustice and war who want to do something about it themselves. For those who can read further, see the "Notes By Chapters."[4]

REINFORCING MORALE BY IDEAS

SINCE SENTIMENTS ARE organized systems of emotion, ideas and impulses to action, believers in this method will want many ideas to build into the structure of their sentiments, to give bones, as it were, to the body of their emotions, and thus make the sentiments enduring and effective. A rich stream of thoughts provides many stimuli to action also, and suggests channels through which energy may usefully move. Also, since gentle resisters meet with much argument and adverse criticism from skeptics and opponents, they need to know thoroughly every aspect and implication of their position and their aims.

Hence it will be highly desirable where possible for at least the leaders to read books and pamphlets on many aspects of nonviolence and pacifism. They may be read by individual members separately, or one member may read them aloud at group meetings. Discussion should follow, with all taking part. If possible, there should be group discussion of all aspects and meanings of nonviolent resistance. The training of the nonviolent resister will be a continuing education. It will be work, exceedingly interesting and good fun.

Having read a fair number of these books and pamphlets or heard them discussed, and having thought them through carefully and discussed them with the members of your group and with all sorts of other people, you will have an understanding of the meaning of creative nonviolent resistance and of your own activities in it. You will have acquired a philosophy of nonviolence that will give you a considerable sureness and guidance for future events. A clear, thorough, well-knit understanding of one's position and aims gives self-confidence and courage. It carries one vigorously through the training period, part of which might otherwise seem monotonous and without much meaning. Such an understanding eliminates inconsistencies of thought and feeling which might cause indecision or be in other ways hampering.

GROUP ORGANIZATION

IN SOME SITUATIONS, there may be a large number of people in a given area who are suffering from some social, economic or political injustice and who want to try organized group nonviolent resistance to end the injustice. It would be a vast help if there were a place where they could meet together for mutual encouragement, and to receive instruction from their leaders in how to proceed, to learn how and why the nonviolent way works, and to practice their responses. Electrical loudspeakers are highly useful. Sometimes such large meetings are the most effective kind of organization.[5] But often small group meetings, along with the large meetings, are helpful, and sometimes where conditions are very harsh, small groups are the only possible kind of organization.

Where, for purposes of training, the small group mode of organization is adopted, these groups should each contain, if possible, not less than five nor more than twelve members. When there are more than twelve, it is very difficult to have free, active and steady discussion. A small group of twelve gets to know one another well and comfortably. They can easily feel strongly as a unit, can think and plan effectively as a unit and can act swiftly, perseveringly and effectively as a unit. More than twelve tend to split up into sub-groups. It is easy for twelve to meet in almost anyone's room or house; a larger number would have to engage a special large room, usually involving expense. Even where the expense would not be a difficulty, the necessity of raising money should be avoided if pos-sible, for sooner or later it becomes a restriction to freedom of thought, will and action. Under totalitarianism, a meeting of twelve or less would not be so likely to attract attention or to be molested as would a larger crowd. Military organization also is based on small units—squads. In construction work small groups of men work more effectively than large ones.[6] Of course the teams or small groups should, as soon as it is feasible, become affiliated with some large local, regional, national or even international organizations whose aims and methods are not inconsistent with those urged here.

CULTIVATING STATES OF MIND

HAVING GOT THEIR GENERAL reading and thinking done, creative believers in nonviolence, both as individuals and in teams, will need to begin the cultivation of the qualities and sentiments which will lead them to take nonviolent action. A few of these states of mind are similar to those of soldiers, but most of them are different. The nonviolent resister will, like soldiers, need courage, self-respect, pa-tience, endurance and the ability to sacrifice himself for a cause. He will need persistence and tenacity in spite of apparent failure, willingness to undergo training, order, and a sense of unity with his fellows. In addition to these qualities, he must, unlike the sol-dier, cultivate an interest in all people, combined with good will and, as far as possible, affection toward them. He must develop his respect for personality, love for truth, tolerance, poise, equanimity, loyalty, humility, hope, and faith in the ultimate fine possibilities of human nature. All of these qualities and sentiments can be culti-vated and strengthened in each one of us.

In both large and small meetings it will be helpful to rehearse in imagination various situations that nonviolent resisters may meet, and then discuss possible tactics of the violent opponents and what should be the reaction and behavior of the nonviolent resister. Non-violent resisters may be faced with either individual or group en-counters by day or by night, with or without onlookers or possible helpers. They may receive anonymous threatening telephone calls or letters, face-to-face threats of violence, rude orders, curses and expressions of derision, contempt, anger and hate. Stones, rotten fruit or glass bottles may be thrown and buildings set on fire, chil-dren threatened or attacked. There may be prolonged persecution, bomb-throwing, shooting of guns, arrests by police, court trials, im-prisonment, even attacks by the military. Sometimes the police would be passive or sympathetic to the violent attackers. All such pos-sibilities should be considered, and in each case some right non-violent response explained, including the reason for it. Each resister singly and all of the resisters together should answer out loud what they will try to do. All this will be a very helpful part of the training.

The practice of nonviolence in small ways should include such matters as always speaking in a low, calm, gentle, evenly pitched tone of voice; exercising patience, self-control and courtesy in all the little daily functions of life; and always trusting the best in other people. Thus one tests and proves to oneself frequently the validity and effectiveness of the method and, like the coral insect, builds in tiny ways the habits that stand like a rock when big crises come.

Attitudes we should rid ourselves of include fear, anger, so-called "righteous indignation," pride, desire for conventional "respectabil-ity" that has no firm moral basis, and desire for power over others.

The psychologists tell us that sentiments are organized systems of feelings, ideas, and impulses to action (instincts). There are numerous ways to stimulate and cultivate feelings or emotions. Ideas can be made to grow by reading, thinking and discussion. Impulses to act can be strengthened by giving them practice and exercise. And there are ways by which all three—emotions, ideas and im-pulses to act—can be woven together and organized into enduring systems of sentiment.

SELF-RESPECT

PERHAPS THE MOST elemental and fundamental of all these inner attitudes is self-respect. Self-respect is the foundation of all moral progress. Without it no one can maintain his morale and purpose in difficult circumstances. We cannot have firmness in action without self-confidence, nor self-confidence without self-respect.

Self-respect and respect from others begin with a simple physical condition: personal cleanliness of body, and cleanliness and neatness of clothes. Gandhi was always insistent on personal cleanliness and neatness and clean, orderly surroundings. The soldier is required to be clean and neat with himself, to polish his boots and shine his buttons, keep his uniform well brushed, and his equipment in good order, not because he will be clean and neat when he is fighting, but in order to create self-respect in him and respect for him among those who see him. We must follow the soldiers in this regard, for we will find ourselves severely criticized by our opponents. In times of stress, they will be likely to accuse us of being disorderly, dirty, ignorant, incompetent, etc. It is a common method of arousing public condemnation. Dirtiness and disorder arouse disgust and from this it is an easy step to use violence against those accused of such faults.

We must not permit such a step to begin. All nonviolent resisters, no matter what their station, must comport themselves so as to create respect among all beholders, as well as self-respect among themselves. We must be able to secure respect from our opponents by every detail of our conduct. We must strive always to keep ourselves, our clothes, our rooms, houses and belongings as clean and neat as is possible under the conditions of our work and location. Yet we should not lose our sense of proportion and devote an undue amount of time to cleaning, to the neglect of other important matters.

A word of warning is necessary at this point; self-respect may degenerate into self-esteem and self-importance. Cleanliness must not become ostentatious, smart, vain or priggish. Military training begins with the inculcation of self-respect, but goes on to the inculcation of pride. The soldier is taught that, as a member of a glorious profession and perhaps of a famous regiment, he is in some way superior to ordinary men. It is drilled into him that he must never do anything to compromise his superiority and that he must not allow other people to question it or smile at it. Everywhere there is a tendency for soldiers to feel that they ought to be placed beyond the reach of laughter; everywhere they show a tendency to take their own dignity and eminence with an excessive seriousness. The nonviolent resister must be on his guard against this tendency. His self-respect must be tempered by a sense of humor. He must be ready to laugh at himself and to be laughed at. Passionately concerned about the success of his cause, he must yet refrain from taking himself too seriously, must avoid the temptation to regard himself as being in any way superior to other men. Humor, including the capacity to laugh at yourself and to accept the laughter of others without resentment, is the characteristic contemporary form of a very ancient virtue, the virtue of humility.

Cleanliness and neatness are not just stuffy, middle-class, respectable virtues. There is a solid biological reason why they have so marked an effect on our self-respect. All animals in their wild state follow the rule of cleanliness. Even scavenger insects like flies are meticulous in frequently cleaning themselves all over.

Keeping clean and neat is a way of saying by your actions that you respect and care so much for human life that you make your immediate environment as favorable as possible to your own form of life and as little favorable as possible to other forms of life, such as germs and flies, which are likely to bring disease, or will at least injure your property, consume some of your sustenance and make life uncomfortable for you. Cleanliness is an elemental and powerful expression of respect for life.

The method of nonviolent resistance needs to be learned by the great mass of people so that they can resist tyranny, oppression or attempted conquest even if their leaders get imprisoned or killed. Since self-respect is the basis of the kind of enduring morale needed for such resistance, we must use every means available for enhancing it. Acquiring self-respect mitigates the resentment that is caused by humiliations, and thus makes self-control easier. That is a great help toward success in using nonviolent resistance.

A second source of self-respect is our conviction of the worthiness of our aims and methods. We can deepen that conviction by progressively mastering more and more of the meaning of our purposes and of our methods. Such conviction also increases courage.

BELIEF IN UNITY OF SPIRIT

WHEN PEOPLE GET TO TALKING about nonviolence they readily admit that in Gandhi's hands it did have power, indeed great power.

Then they usually say, "But he was a saint, and I am not." Or, "I haven't such courage or selflessness or strength." Or, "That is asking too much of the average man."

In pondering on this, consider Prime Minister Disraeli's reported saying that "anything you truly believe in is practical" and Gandhi's frequent statement that successful nonviolent resistance requires a firm belief in God. From his firm belief in God came his firm belief in nonviolent resistance.

People who do not believe in God or who dislike references to what they call supernatural should know that Gandhi said that God is another name for Truth. Truth and God, he said, are the same. Instead of Truth, some people would prefer the term Ultimate Reality or Unity or Spirit. Moslems would prefer the name Allah; Hindus might use the name Brahma or Shiva or Rama; Buddhists of different schools might use still other names or no name at all. We need not quarrel over the name. We know that Gandhi was referring to a supreme intangible Power, and that success in nonviolent resistance requires a firm belief in such a Power.

How are firm beliefs acquired? One method is through prolonged experience. We all believe, for instance, in the force of gravitation. We all began experiencing it as soon as we were born. When each baby lies on its back and waves its arms and legs around, it is experimenting with the force of gravitation. Later, when it tries to walk and finally succeeds, it is experimenting with and learning about that force. When it plays with stones or blocks and learns to put one object on top of another, it learns more about the power and constancy of gravity. As a result of all this, every one of us profoundly believes in the force of gravity and always tries to act consistently with it in every movement of his body.

CONTROLLED EXPERIMENT IN THE POWER OF LOVE

THERE IS ANOTHER way to get firm belief—by a deliberate, planned series of experiences. This is the scientific method of experimentation with careful control of conditions and recording of results. The application of scientific method always begins with a hypothesis, a conscious guess or question, followed by experiments to test its truth or validity. Sometimes it is a rationally conceived possible correlation. When the scientific method is carefully carried out and tested by many observers, it usually ends with an equally firm belief. An instance is the present-day belief in the reality and usefulness of radio waves.

Most scientists restrict their experiments to the material world of space and time. Gandhi extended the use of the scientific method to the realm of intangible, subtle human relationships, the realm of morals and of what is called spirit.

He had a hypothesis, an assumption, an intuition, that the spirit or essence of human unity—or if you prefer the name, God— exists, is present always and everywhere in all human hearts as well as transcending the whole world, and that it is supremely powerful. He proceeded to test this hypothesis every day, and year after year. He stated his belief that truth and God are synonymous. He entitled his autobiography, *The Story of My Experiments with Truth.* He might have called it "My Experiments with the Divine Spirit," or "My Experiments with Human Unity." The result of his incessant experiments was an unshakable belief and trust in God, and in the power of God acting in all men, and hence in the power of non-violence.

One essential feature of the scientific method is that the experiments must be capable of repetition by any other scientist who is willing to follow the same conditions, and the results must be substantially the same.

Gandhi's application of scientific method was in the realm of living forces. One of the features of living forces, what might almost be called a law, is that all life responds to suitable stimuli, and that the kind of response called growth depends on many, many, many repetitions of stimuli that are tiny—what in the moral realm we would call gentle. Gandhi recognized and practiced this law. For over fifty years all his teaching and action consisted of many, many repetitions of gentle, loving stimuli to the spirit in the hearts of all men, including his opponents. He thus caused the seed of the spirit in the hearts of almost everyone to sprout and grow and finally in many cases to govern their actions.

It is true that there were some apparent failures. That happens in laboratory experiments, too. But the successes were so many and so striking that all those who are sensitive to the development of fine human relations have been deeply impressed.

Of course there are many skeptics who are scornful of or simply not interested in a hypothesis that there is an intangible, living power that can be thus invoked and used by men. Their skepticism is not supported, however, by the feature of intangibility, for radio waves have that quality, and nobody denies the power of radio waves. There are certain real, enduring and powerful forces in men that are immeasurable and living. The belief of the Jews that they were chosen by God has sustained them through centuries of oppression. Other examples are the Englishman's sense of superiority, and the idea of many scientists that man is master of nature.

If nature is the realm of space and time, then the word "super-natural" can no longer be used incredulously or as outmoded and a sign of superstition, because such scientists as Einstein, Heisenberg, Jeans, Weyl, Bridgman, de Broglie and Dingle have stated categorically that the laws of space and time do not apply to the nuclear forces of the atom. Something as real as the hydrogen bomb transcends space and time. There are forces now recognized by science which are, if you please, supernatural.

Hence it no longer seems unreasonable, fantastic, superstitious or unscientific to believe that there may be an intangible, trans-natural, living power in the hearts of all men. Be skeptical if you wish, but don't be bigoted in your skepticism. After all, nowadays scientific laws are regarded by scientists as only statements of strong probability. It is unscientific to say dogmatically that something simply cannot be.

The present extreme dangers for all mankind are due primarily to defective human relations enlarged into international scope—to such attitudes as fear, suspicion, anger, pride, selfishness, greed and lust for power. It has become imperative to experiment with finer forces and influences in this realm—such forces as a frank admission by each person and each nation that we are all human and have made mistakes, such attitudes as forgiveness, willingness to take risks for a fine end, trust, and even that power called Love.

Let us be profoundly scientific and expand the area for experiment! I am not for the purposes of this point urging you to believe in God or nonviolence, or to love everybody or indeed anybody. I am only suggesting that you do some serious experimenting in a realm you are not already familiar with, to do research that may prove highly profitable for you, for your descendants, for your nation and the world. Maybe you can thus acquire a firm belief in an intangible force that is new to you.

Why do you not *today,* just out of scientific curiosity, begin some little private experiments with, for example, such a principle as "Do unto others as you would have them do unto you." Try it at least fifty times, and keep a record of the results. If they are generally favorable, go on from there.

STEPS TO UNITY WITH FELLOW MEN

THE NEXT MOST IMPORTANT thing to cultivate is the sentiment of unity with all mankind. That includes opponents—whether of another nation, race, class, religion, economic or political party. Such a sense of unity must begin in relation to those near at hand, familiar and friendly, and then be broadened to include strangers, opponents and distant people.

GET UNITY BY SINGING TOGETHER. There are several ways in which this sense of unity, at first with your own group, can be developed. The first means of developing this is by singing together. Grundtvig, the great Danish educator, had the students in the folk high schools begin every day, every class and every meal with joint singing of folk songs and ballads. The practice has been kept up and has been a powerful influence in creating a strong, healthy community spirit among the Danes.[7] Soldiers know this is true. So do college students, church members and everyone who has ever sung in chorus with others.

Music is a subtle influence but very powerful. Ruskin said, "The four necessities of life are food, shelter, raiment and music," and the history of mankind bears him out. Music stirs our emotions deeply, gives form to our feelings, helps us to understand the life of feeling, educates our feelings, stimulates our imagination, helps to solve inner conflicts, enriches our consciousness, brings about subtle and profound inner integrations of character, and expresses feelings and sympathies which cannot be put into words or even into acts. When group singing is done with skill and intelligent care, it develops activity of ear and mind together, quickness of decision and accuracy of perception and of thinking. The power of rhythmic coordination that it develops is important. Making music in a social group gives self-assurance, vigor, unity, a sense of equality, happiness, love of beauty, an awareness of making a significant contribution to the group.[8] The wise civilizations of the Greeks and Chinese strongly emphasized the importance of music.

Practically everybody can sing. It costs nothing and calls for no special equipment. As to the kind of music to be sung, I advise folk songs, ballads and Negro spirituals. They are simple, within the range of every voice, vigorous, expressive of feelings close to the heart of everyone, and beautiful.[9] If some groups composed entirely of church members desire to sing hymns sometimes, let them choose only those whose words are free from doubt, fear, trouble, pride or warlike connotation.[10] If any member of a team of nonviolent resisters prefers not to have hymns, it will be best to stick to folk songs.

GET UNITY BY FOLK DANCING OR RHYTHMIC EXERCISES TOGETHER. Another means of developing a strong sense of unity in the group is folk dancing. It requires some space indoors or outdoors, and instrumental music, phonograph records or radio music, and so perhaps would not be possible for many teams. Yet the experience of vigorous movement in rhythmic unison with others, to the sound of music, produces in the individual an improved coordination of mind and body, a development of power to receive and act upon suggestion, a sense of number, measure, order, accuracy, skill, proportion and rhythm. Dancing produces a heightening of emotions, a fusion of sense and spirit, and a feeling of liberation, spontaneity and joy. It is a mode of music in which our bodies are the instruments and media of expression. It increases one's self-control, poise, assuredness and courage. It gives to all who participate in it a peculiarly personal, vivid, strong and enduring sense of unity, of harmony and concord, of mutual coordination, and of the proper subordination of parts to the whole.[11] It is similar to military marching in these respects, but it is superior and more effective.

Folk dancing is completely different from formal society dancing by twos—in form, feeling and result. Folk dancing is found in practically all nations and races, and it is an important part of any healthy culture. In practically all early communities, folk songs and folk dancing were important means of cultivating and maintaining a strong sense of unity and community. Since believers in gentleness are trying to create a new and better civilization, they will be wise to utilize the means whose effectiveness has been so thoroughly tested and proved.[12]

If some believers in nonviolence dislike the idea of folk dancing because they think it is "arty" or affected, they should remember that sturdy, vigorous, brave, unaffected, unselfconscious men and women among peasants and savages of all countries have always danced folk dances a great deal and still continue to do so. Highly cultured people like the Greeks did it. In America we still have our Appalachian and Ozark highlanders and Indians doing such dances as a natural part of their lives. So it is only our modern opinions that deserve doubt, not the dancing itself. If it is self-consciousness that makes you hesitate, try folk dancing once in earnest, and you will find that, in the zest of the dance, your self-consciousness ends once and for all. In this respect, too, folk dancing differs from modern round dances.

OTHER MEANS TO UNITY

OTHER SIMPLE AIDS to group unity will be occasional walks together and periodical light refreshments or simple meals together if the financing of them can be arranged. The sharing of food as a symbol and stimulus to unity goes back very far in human history. The mess-rooms of the army are the places where much of its morale is made. Certain group games, not too competitive, are also good.

UNITY BY JOINT MEDITATION. For some people, still another means of gaining a deep sense of unity is the practice of periodically sitting together in silent meditation for not less than fifteen minutes and preferably for half an hour or even longer. There are perhaps two modes of doing this which will prove useful. In one, a single idea or sentiment (*e.g.,* courage, or an incident in the life of some great exemplar of nonviolence) is chosen, and all the members of the team concentrate their thoughts on it. In the other, the team members try to dismiss from their minds all thinking or attention to sense impressions and wait in silence. When done rightly and free from distractions, there takes place an inner integration, a reunion between the superficial and the deeper levels of the mind, a silent growth of imagination, of sensibility, of organic emotional relationships, of common apprehension, common sentiment and common purpose, a development of a deeper understanding and appreciation of the values we hold together. Sometimes the group may choose to pursue one of these kinds of meditation, sometimes the other. Remember that what takes place is an organic growth of these intangible qualities and processes. Growth takes considerable time, and requires patience and many repetitions of gentle stimuli and quiet opportunities. Such corporate silent meditation eventually creates among the team members a unity at a deeper level than that which comes from the other methods mentioned.

Complete silence should be observed during the entire time. The ending of the meditation period had best be left to the team leader, who can indicate it by rising or by some other appropriate gesture.

Individual members can of course meditate by themselves, if they desire.

The unity and sense of common purpose and common values developed by these methods will of course make a team far more effective in both joint and individual action. That is why, in the army, so much time and detailed care is taken to instill a strong sense of unity in each squad, platoon, company and regiment. Danger and hardship are not as hard for most people to bear as a sense of isolation from one's fellow men, whether the isolation is real or only fancied, or caused only by the actions of others. One of the hardest things which conscientious objectors during the world wars had to bear was a feeling of loneliness, a feeling that nobody agreed with them or cared about them. This was enhanced in some cases by separate confinement in prison. Nonviolent resisters will be wise to prepare themselves, so that they will not suffer from the hardship of that feeling.

A strong sense of unity gives a feeling of mutual support and power, and hence it is a great factor in creating courage and endurance. It also promotes kindliness and tolerance. By choosing for meditation such themes as tolerance, the unity of all mankind and love for all people, the sense of unity will be widened. Such an extension of feeling and thinking can also be aided by suitable reading, and by the action described below.[13] Much can be gained by trying to understand human character and how it works. Instead of the much-abused term "love," we may say "interest-affection." As Gerald Heard has said, when you become intensely interested in a person you can't help coming to be affected by him and feel affection toward him; and if you have affection for a person you are inevitably interested in him. Human nature, even when at first sight repellant, is always interesting if it is closely and intelligently observed.

GETTING MORALE BY HEARING TRADITION AND STORIES OF HEROIC ACHIEVEMENT. The British Brigadier-General, F. P. Crozier, speaking out of his remarkable experience in training raw recruits for battle in World War I, said that the most potent element in raising and maintaining the morale and effectiveness of troops is to tell them the traditions of the regiment, its great exploits and deeds of heroism in days gone by. Tradition, story and example are wonderfully potent forces to develop initiative and rouse energy. Perhaps one reason for this is indicated by the fact that our dreams are in story form, about events that affect ourselves or other people. This suggests that our subconscious minds think in story form. Hence, stories appeal to our entire personalities—the subconscious as well as the consciously thinking and feeling part. A constantly held mental image of an ideal or heroic historical person probably helps us also to choose wise means in seeking our goal.

In preparing nonviolent resisters for their form of action, it will therefore be important to read aloud or tell at team meetings the lives and sayings of great heroes and exemplars of nonviolence.[14] Also of value are individual incidents or examples of nonviolent resistance shown by all sorts of people.[15] See the "Notes By Chapters" for source references. Reading aloud or reciting great poetry will also deepen, heighten and enrich the emotions, illuminate the understanding and stir energy for action. All such reading will want to be followed by discussion to clarify and strengthen the common thinking and understanding of the team.

COURAGE

COURAGE WILL DEVELOP as the sense of unity grows under all the exercises described above, and from the work for others described later. It is enhanced by the growth of self-respect, and by voluntary simplicity of living. Another help is reading or hearing stories of great deeds of courage and the lives of brave men, especially the deeds and lives and words of great nonviolent resisters. Reading and reciting poetry of action is good. A study of the history of the peace movement will give a sense of historical continuity and momentum, of being one of a great company of believers in a significant idea.[16] This promotes courage, patience and endurance. A love of truth is a strong aid to courage. Good health is an aid, though not so important as others. Meditation and, for those who are religious, prayer are great aids to developing a sense of the reality, power and eternity of intangible moral and spiritual forces, and a realization that each of us shares in those forces. Such realizations give great courage. A thorough understanding of our principles, methods and purposes, and a deep conviction of their worth will give us fortitude.

ACTION

At this point, critics might object that the development of intangible states of mind which we have been considering is not going to produce action but sentimentalism, irresponsibility, empty, idealistic wordiness and quietism. As we have already seen, however, a great part of the training of soldiers—men primarily of action—is largely for the purpose of creating inner states of mind, emotion and will. Polishing buttons and boots and brushing the uniform is done to build self-respect. Close-order drill, which in itself has little if any combat value, creates a sense of unity and subordination and a habit of complete obedience. And regimental deeds and traditions are recounted in order to develop group pride or "esprit de corps," based on emulation of the demonstrated courage and battle-eagerness shown by soldiers of the same unit in the past.[17]

It is true that if training stopped with what we have been discussing, it would probably result in sentimentality, weakness and eventually futile quietism. The soldier, in addition to the training we have mentioned, has to practice manipulation of weapons and shooting, the very things which he will do in war. He will practice by doing with inanimate targets what in actual combat will kill people and accomplish the objects of war. He must develop skill in the actions which he will have to perform in battle, or as near an imitation as is possible.

So it must be with the nonviolent resister. His purpose—persuasion—is not accomplished with bullets, shells, poison gas, bayonets and lying propaganda, but with deeds that will prove to all people—neutrals and opponents—that he is truthful, trustworthy, self-controlled, kind, courageous, respectful of all personality, nonviolent, just, persistent—in short, that he is the kind of citizen who wins the respect, trust, admiration and affection of all men. He must become the kind of person whom governments must treat with respect in order to maintain their own prestige in the eyes of the world and of their own supporters. Such virtues can be cultivated and proven only by deeds. Actions speak louder than words. If nonviolent resisters act to prove themselves enduringly possessed of such character, then they will be mightily persuasive against any and all opponents, even against prejudiced, hard and cruel people. The persistent, voluntary, repeated nonviolent sufferings of such resisters will arouse the support of worldwide public opinion, will upset the morale of any opponent and convert the hardest foe.

TRAINING BY DEEDS

THIS MEANS, THEN, THAT the training of nonviolent resisters must be crowned with a program of deeds that will prove the resisters' good citizenship, discipline and unselfish devotion to the welfare of the community and commonwealth to which they belong. They must be active in healing all sorts of defects in our society, and in creating justice, in such a way as to win the strong support of public opinion.

Unless their training includes action of the kind that will occur in their subsequent actual struggles to build a better world and to solve conflicts, they and their organizations, like so many pacifist groups, will be doomed to sentimentalism, failure, quietism and probable eventual reaction. Just as sentiment stimulates and guides action, so does habitual right action build up and invigorate right sentiment. Action and sentiment always go together and interact.[18] Such action will not be just educational and aimed at the future. It begins here and now to remedy actual cases of injustice, to build up new and better conditions, to exemplify human unity.

MANUAL WORK. The beginning of action adequate to our problem is manual work. Something all members of a team can work at together would be best, and that will be a service to the community. In many neighborhoods there are churches, schools or individual homes that need repairs or painting. I know one middle-class suburban community near Philadelphia where the parents, working with their own hands, built a school for their children. In some vacant lots there may be much unsightly trash or low spots that fill with rainwater and become breeding places for mosquitoes. Some streets are littered with papers, tin cans, old bottles and other trash. There are trenches to be dug, roads to be built or repaired, gardens to be weeded, many kinds of hand work. If believers in constructive, loving nonviolence will give their labor regularly and steadily to such repairs, sanitation work and cleaning-up, they will promote both individual and community morale and good feeling. The work-service camps of the Mennonites, Quakers, International Voluntary Service and *Eirene* are examples of this sort. But if for any individual or family such work is not possible, then some manual work at home—cooking, preparing food for cooking, sweeping, scrubbing floors, dusting furniture, making beds, mending clothes, darning stockings, knitting, mending furniture, cleaning up the yard or area, working in the garden, reducing sources for breeding of flies, carrying coal and water, washing windows, dishes and clothes, and helping the neighbors in like fashion—any of the thousand-and-one things that constantly need doing. Some of them are light and easy enough for even invalids or the aged or children to do. Some, like knitting, can be done at odd times, or while other duties or talk are going on. Men should get over the foolish idea that it is not fitting or is beneath their dignity to do any of such things.

REASONS FOR MANUAL WORK. Very early in the development of the human embryo, a nerve grows out from the spinal cord to the hand and fingers. It is the second nerve to grow from the central nervous system, the first one going to the region of the mouth and face. In the evolution of mankind, when man's thumb had attained its present position on the hand so that the creature could grasp stones or sticks, he used them as tools or weapons. Thus the effectiveness of his limbs was extended and he began to deal more efficiently with his environment. He began to meet problems. He learned to experiment and think in order to solve them. Thus, early in man's evolution, his hands were closely related to his brain and mind.[19] The development of the mind has always been closely conected with and dependent on the increasing skill of the hand. The early stone-age tools that have been found indicate that man has been using tools with his hands for at least 100,000 years.

Again, the sense of touch, which is so delicate in the hand, is closely connected with and expressive of human sympathy.[20] To express sympathy one instinctively touches a person who is in deep trouble, or a person whom one loves. So a movement based on a re-establishment of human unity will naturally find an important elemental part of its expression through the hand.

The articular (joint) sensations, especially of the hand, together with the sense of touch, give peculiarly intimate and vivid experience and knowledge, so that education which has a strong element of manual work in it is usually powerful, sure and substantial.[21]

For all the hundreds of thousands of years that man has lived on this earth he has engaged in manual work. As a result, there has developed an intimate, close and unbreakable interaction between manual work and man's moral character. The past two and a half centuries of machinery have not broken this connection. Man *needs* hand work to maintain his happiness and sanity. One evidence of this is the recent impressive development in America of "hobbies," home work shops, and "do-it-yourself" devices among office workers, professionals and intellectuals. They are hungry for it.

Habitual voluntary bodily activities, especially those of the hands, build self-respect, self-confidence, self-reliance, courage, hope, sound and independent judgment, patience, tenacity and endurance. There are four convincing examples of this: 1.) Military discipline, which we have already mentioned, develops these qualities in the most ordinary human material. Its effectiveness in this respect has been proved for ages. 2.) The ruling groups in almost every country teach their children before the age of ten, while they are sensitive to influences, to ride horseback and play games, and they themselves continue to ride horseback and play games such as tennis and golf which require great manual skill. For thousands of years they have done this, not just for fun or prestige, but because they are keenly aware of the effect of bodily skills in creating the intangible qualities of character mentioned above which are so necessary for the organizers and rulers of society. They are also necessary for all the citizens in a democracy. 3.) Mental hospitals use manual work, which they call "occupational therapy" to restore to normal health and sanity the patients who are deeply melancholy, despairing and lacking in self-confidence. 4.) Madame Montessori's discovery and practice of the curative and stimulating effects of developing skills of the hand in little children.

It is true that millions of people have done nothing but manual work all their lives and yet have not shown the qualities of self-confidence, self-respect, self-reliance, hope, courage and the independent strength that comes from them. But the reason for that failure is that extreme, prolonged poverty, unemployment, disease, exploitation, social degradation, lack of unity, and especially inability to see any way out of this nightmare have taken the heart out of the victims and sapped those fine qualities of character as fast as they have been built up. But organized, disciplined nonviolent resistance supplies the inspiration, hope and method that permits and develops the steady growth of unified strength.

Work with the hands gives immediate and tangible results. It causes a prompt, perceptible change in one's thinking and feeling. It therefore gives an immediate sense of accomplishment and satisfaction, and the encouragement to do it again and continue so as to win still further concrete results. It is self-validating. It provides the sort of stimulus to thought and feeling that all people respond to, no matter what their book education, previous experience or position in society.

Regular, free, creative, manual work as part of a program of social and economic change tends to mollify or prevent bitterness and anger, which are repellent and wasteful.

In a prolonged struggle, such as the interracial one for example, after a particularly severe bout there may be among the nonviolent resisters a let-down due to moral fatigue. A struggle of nonviolent resistance is a vigorous assertion of the moral and spiritual unity of mankind, carried on not only against the opposition of the opponent and the lethargy, reluctance to think, and habits of feeling and thinking of the general public, but also against the evidence of our senses that we are all different from one another and our prevailing assumption that these differences are of greatest importance. To struggle against all this opposition for a long while is morally tiring.

For this reason, some critics have said that nonviolent resistance is not practical because it asks too much of human nature. They argue that it keeps its followers on moral tiptoe too long, and there would therefore inevitably be a disastrous reaction, a slump of moral behavior. This is the reason why Gandhi, in the intervals between active struggles with the British Government, always resorted to the promotion of hand spinning and other village industries, and other items of his constructive economic and social program. He knew that hand work is deeply restful, healing and curative, and a subtle and indirect way of asserting our common human nature.

Regular manual work will act as a corrective to any members who might tend to become sentimental about the training or about the tasks ahead.

We must work *with* people as well as *for* them, and best of all, help them to help themselves. Giving money is not enough, nor is it at all an equivalent for actual manual work.

If all kinds of people—the manual workers, the unemployed, the middle class, the intellectuals and the rich—can take part in manual labor, it will provide a common experience and be a symbol of democratic common endeavor and of a bridging of the gap between the classes. It will help to unite leaders and followers. Such work is something that everyone can do, young and old, men and women, sick and well, crippled and whole, strong and weak, new converts and old believers, skilled and unskilled, city dwellers and country people, rich and poor, educated and ignorant. In some form it can be done at all seasons of the year, in all kinds of weather, by day or by night, and in almost every place.

Not everyone can make speeches, and everlasting listening to speeches eventually may become emotional and intellectual debauchery and get us nowhere. Manual work is not passive, but active and creative. The creation of something tangible and useful creates self-respect and self-reliance. The seeming smallness of accomplishment at any one occasion does not make it insignificant. Our physical bodies and the body of society are built up slowly, cell by cell, and each cell is important.

OTHER MODES OF SERVICE

THERE ARE OTHER concrete expressions of the sentiments of unity and respect for personality which creative pacifists will want to engage in. Among these are visiting and helping men in prison, aiding in the great problems of crime prevention and aid to discharged prisoners; helping the poorest people; visiting and helping the sick, whether in hospitals, municipal houses or private homes; removal of injustices to members of any minority groups; recreation and education for children; adult education; care of the aged; public health and sanitation work; education of mothers in prenatal clinics; and care of the insane and the feeble-minded. Different members of the nonviolent team will have different aptitudes and will be attracted toward different ones of these tasks. Teams from different areas may organize and distribute such work among themselves.

It would probably be wise for all nonviolent resisters to get training in First Aid. Then whenever there is an accident, fire, flood, explosion, riot or other violence they would not have to stand by helplessly, but could be of immediate use.

Of course I do not mean that everyone must drop what he is doing and turn entirely to the work above described. But these are the kinds of things that people who want to work effectively for peace and social justice should do. Whatever time they do have for such work outside of the team meetings should be applied in these ways. Some people can give their vacations or holidays to this work. Some will have to give their whole time to it. Surely a true creative peace in which kindness and justice are always predominant is a sufficiently fine ideal to call for great sacrifices, greater even than war demands.

The chief goals must be the achievement of truth, justice and human unity. That old-fashioned sentiment called love of people must be the chief motive. Only this, used intelligently in nonviolent resistance, can purge us of our own selfishnesses and mistakes and convert our opponents to a new position and thus win a permanent solution of each conflict as it arises.

Such constructive work will also help to prevent or mitigate the kind of crisis in which voluntary suffering becomes the nonviolent resister's hard lot.

A DEMOCRATIC METHOD. The disciplines and activities described here do not stifle initiative or spontaneity as military drill does. Hence these disciplines need not be mistrusted by lovers of freedom. We have seen that the method of nonviolent resistance is wholly democratic and purely persuasive. It will make impossible any dictatorships, whether of the Right or Left, of aristocracy or proletariat, of the wealthy or the military. It leaves the initiative to individuals where it psychologically and necessarily must be. But it develops an effective mass veto to all policies which the people have come to believe are harmful.

WE MUST DIG DEEP

WAR OR VIOLENCE is no simple excrescence that can be removed merely by having large numbers of people petition the government or simply refuse to fight, or by passing legislation. Such distinguished authorities as the British Major-General Sir F. Maurice from the military; the English Conservative editor, J. L. Garvin from the Right; John Dewey, the American philosopher and educationist, from the Center; and Lenin from the Left, have all stated that war is an integral part and inevitable result of the kind of society in which we live.[22] If this is true, and many agree that it is, we must, in order to prevent war, democratically and without violence, change that society from its very foundations and throughout its entire structure and motivation.

The program described in this chapter is not proposed as a complete, simplified pattern for the social, economic and political activities of society. Rather it is a means of building up a conscious purpose and practice of mutuality and friendly cooperation. It is a method of increasing social integration, of enlarging the opportunities for effectively taking part in the total life of the community. It is a way of correlating fine means with fine ends. It is a way of developing the sentiments, motives, mutual trust and moral power needed to carry us without violence through the vast changes that are coming so swiftly, a way to make a beginning of effective, remedial economic action, to bring about wise changes, and to support the new forms of society and assure that they will be better than what we now have. Others can formulate the detailed technical economic and political changes required from time to time. We must build a much stronger moral foundation for society than we now have.

To end war and violence means having a better world, but that is impossible unless the people in it grow better. No relationship is finer than the people who compose it. Those who are endeavoring to abolish war, therefore, must themselves strive hard to become better people by living better lives. Even if one says that it is the evil framework of society that must be changed before the mass of people can become better, it remains true that, in order to gain sufficient influence, trust and power to win a big following and cause the change, the leaders who aspire to alter that bad social system must themselves become better men and women than they were before. And they must continue that progress and remain humble in order that when they attain power they do not become corrupted and sell out the cause. Only the method of nonviolence can be proof against such corruption.

We have more control over our own characters than we have over the external forms of society. So we must begin with ourselves, knowing that to the extent that we can win self-control and strength in the qualities needed for this struggle, we will be able to begin to modify society. Indeed, that part of society in our own neighborhood will begin to change as soon as we start. The responsibility thus rests squarely on ourselves and our work begins there. We must change the character of our own lives. This means for each of us a new and morally better way of life, to be developed gradually yet continuously, just as any new habit is learned. The disciplines described above are ways by which people in groups can acquire the habit of nonviolence so strongly that they will be able to prove its power, endure any opposition and attack, and create a finer social order.

NOT A DOGMATIC FORMULA FOR SOCIETY BUT A METHOD OF WINNING POWER

WE CANNOT FORESEE the exact economic and political forms of society that will come from the sustained and thorough application of the principle of nonviolent resistance with its adjuncts. Human nature and society are too vast and complex, and social change these days is too swift to make it possible to draft in advance a detailed architectural plan of that sort and then put it into effect. Not even the Russian communists adhered steadily to their original plan, and they have used violence. But we may be sure that the method of nonviolent persuasion, because of its inherent qualities, will, by its application, bring about a more just, finer and happier world.

When the scientific method was first begun, the early scientists, such as Galileo, Roger Bacon and others, had no idea what kind of a world would come from its use. They knew it was a powerful method for discovering truth about the physical world. They trusted it, and they and their followers have applied it with amazing results within its sphere. Similarly with the method of nonviolent persuasion. It cannot help producing fine results in the human world.

The structure of a society grows inevitably out of its activities, because not only is the structure a summation, a result of a long accumulation of those activities, but also the structure and the activities are both of them *events*. At any instant during the life of the structure, it seems to be permanent, while the activities are fleeting and changing. But regarded in a longer time-scale, or after the structure has ceased to exist except in memory, the structure too is seen to be only an event. Structure changes slowly and activities or functions change quickly, but both are events.[23]

It is the same with means and ends. Both are events. The end is a summation of all the means used in reaching it, and the character of the end cannot help being settled by the character of the means. This gives us immense hope, for the means are here and now and subject to our choice and within our power and control. The only way to improve the future is to improve the present by using a sound method, and keep on applying that method day after day.[24] If we choose a fine means and persist in it, we can be certain of reaching a fine end.

I grant that we all feel a deep need for a sense of direction and orientation, and that we like to see our goal clearly. Yet maybe the chief function of a mental image of an ideal goal is to maintain our persistence in working toward it but not otherwise to strengthen our wills or ensure our achievement. The character of the means we use determines the end that we actually come to, far more than our advance picture of the ideal goal determines it. Profound and careful thinking and planning we certainly need, but to plan further than our control extends is illusory and futile. In social processes, where the forces are infinitely complex but slightly known and unpredictable, only the near goals can be clear goals. And only clear goals can be effective to guide action.[25] Our direction lies mainly in our method, though we may also, if we desire, choose certain definite nearby objectives. One step at a time. For these reasons, nonviolent persuasion is not hitched to any particular "ism" or rigid economic or political doctrine. It is a method, not a dogma. Yet being a method of persuasion and of gaining power, it may be used to put into effect any particular program which the people want, provided that program is itself fully consistent with nonviolence.

These suggestions are only a beginning. Select from them those which you can use. They are an adaptation of the discipline devised and used by Gandhi, the greatest modern exemplar of the method. Practically every one of these suggestions has been a successful element in some established professional or cultural discipline. The sum of the different parts of such training is more moral and deeper and will become more effective than military discipline. This new discipline, like all others, will evolve and become more efficient.

At present, man is the only animal that makes organized war on its own species. To argue, as some pessimists and many militarists do, that man can never act otherwise, is to assert that man is less intelligent and less capable of self-control than any other animal, most insects, or any microscopic form of life. This I cannot believe. Nor can I believe that, although man has worked out a highly effective discipline for mass murder, he is incapable of evolving an effective discipline for powerful mass nonviolence and its resulting mutual aid and benefit. Man, who has conquered space with his airplane, rocket and radio, and time with his languages and printing, who has learned through the processes of life, chemistry and physics to breed vegetables and animals with new qualities, can and will learn how to control himself and direct society to fine ends. If Western civilization fails at the task, and if human life somewhere on the planet endures, the task will be accomplished by other cultures.

Toward the close of a life of wide, keen observation and deep discriminative thinking, Plato said, in effect, that persuasion is at the basis of the order of the world.[26] Profoundly wise men of many civilizations have said in various ways that man has in him the spark and possibility of divinity. A great and successful exemplar of nonviolent resistance said that we should change our minds completely, and that we should seek first the Kingdom of God and His righteousness, that the Kingdom of God is at hand, and that the true followers of the spirit shall do greater things than he did. With what we know, these words, spoken at a time when the outlook was dark, should encourage us to go forward in firm hope.

NOTES BY CHAPTERS

CHAPTER ONE

[1] See A. Fenner Brockway, *Non-cooperation in Other Lands* (Madras, India: Tagore & Co.); also Brockway, "Does Non-cooperation Work," in Devere Allen (ed.), *Pacifism in the Modern World* (New York: Doubleday, Doran 1929).

[2] See Mohandas K. Gandhi, *Satyagraha in South Africa* (Ahmedabad, India: Navijivan 1950); *The Story of My Experiments with Truth* (Boston, Mass.: Beacon Press 1957).

[3] See Gandhi, *The Story of My Experiments with Truth,* above cited.

[4] See Rajendra Prasad, *Satyagraha in Champaran* (Ahmedabad, India: Navajivan 1940); Gandhi, *The Story of My Experiments with Truth,* above cited; Mahadev Desai, *The Epic of Travancore* (Ahmedabad: Navajivan 1930).

[5] S. E. Stokes, *Essays Political and National* (Madras, India: S. Ganesan 1921).

[6] See Mahadev Desai, *The Story of Bardoli* (Ahmedabad, India: Navajivan 1929).

[7] See C. F. Andrews, *Mahatma Gandhi's Ideas* (New York: Macmillan 1930).

[8] See Joan V. Bondurant, *Conquest of Violence* (Princeton, N. J.: Princeton Univ. Press 1958).

[9] See Philip Friedman, *Their Brothers Keepers* (New York: Crown 1957).

[10] See press dispatches as follows: A. P. March 24, 1943; Sept. 25, 1944; Aug. 31, 1943; Oct. 11, 1942. U. P. May 5, 1943; Dec. 9, 1940. Also *The New York Times,* Aug. 20, 1943; April 21, 1947 (obituary of King Christian); *New York Herald-Tribune,* dispatch by Marquis Childs, May 14, 1943; *The Call,* Nov. 20, 1942, dispatch from John Lester Levine. Also Philip Friedman, *Their Brother's Keepers,* pp. 149-158, above cited.

[11] Gene Sharp, *Tyranny Could Not Quell Them* (London: Publication Com. of Peace News 1959).

[12] See Gene Sharp, "Kirkenes Journey," in *Peace News* (London), Jan. 31, Feb. 7, 14, 21, 28 and Mar. 7, 14, 21, 28 and April 4 and 19, 1948. Also Diderich H. Lund, "Pacifism Under the Occupation," in *Fellowship* (Nyack, N. Y.) December 1948; Sharp, *Tyranny Could Not Quell Them,* above cited.

[13] See Martin Luther King Jr., *Stride Toward Freedom* (New York: Harper 1958); Chester Bowles, "What Negroes Can Learn from Gandhi," *Saturday Evening Post,* March 1, 1958; L. D. Reddick, "The Bus Boycott in Montgomery," in *Voices of Dissent* (New York: Grove Press 1958); various articles in *Liberation* and *Fellowship,* 1956-57. For a concise pictorial account, see *Martin Luther King and the Montgomery Story* (Nyack, N. Y.: Fellowship of Reconciliation).

For examples of nonviolence in personal life, see the New Testament and the life of Buddha, for instance in Edwin Arnold, *The Light of Asia* (London:

Trübner 1885). Also, A. Ruth Fry, *Victories Without Violence* (London: Dennis Dobson 1952); Allan A. Hunter, *Courage in Both Hands* (New York: Fellowship 1951); and *Christians in the Arena* (Nyack, N. Y.: Fellowship 1958).

Additional titles of interest and relevance may be found in *Bibliography of Books on War, Pacifism, Nonviolence and Related Studies* (Nyack, N. Y.: Fellowship 1959). Many books currently in print by or about Gandhi are published by Navajivan Publishing House, Ahmedabad, India, and are obtainable from the American Friends Service Committee, 20 South 12th Street, Philadelphia 7, Pa.

CHAPTER TWO

[1] F. C. Bartlett, *Psychology and the Soldier*, p. 175 (Cambridge: Cambridge Univ. Press 1927).

[2] See A. F. Shand, *The Foundations of Character*, p. 448 (New York: Macmillan 1914).

[3] See W. B. Cannon, *Bodily Changes in Pain, Hunger, Fear and Rage* (New York: Appleton 1927).

[4] See G. W. Crile, *Origin and Nature of the Emotions*, esp. pp. 30, 52, 61 (Philadelphia: W. B. Saunders 1915). Also William Ernest Hocking, *Morale and Its Enemies*, p. 53f. (New Haven: Yale Univ. Press 1918).

[5] See T. Burrow, *The Social Basis of Consciousness* (New York: Harcourt Brace 1927).

[6] See Baudouin, *Suggestion and Auto-Suggestion*, p. 143 (New York: Dodd, Mead 1931).

[7] See William Ernest Hocking, *Human Nature and Its Remaking*, 2nd ed., p. 374 (New Haven: Yale Univ. Press 1928).

[8] Shand, above cited, pp. 430, 448.

[9] See Erich Fromm, *The Art of Loving* (New York: Harper 1957), for his conception of self-love.

[10] See E. J. Kempf, *Autonomic Functions and the Personality*, pp. 93ff. (New York: Nervous and Mental Diseases Publishing Co. 1921). Also W. Trotter, *Instincts of the Herd in Peace and War* (New York: Macmillan 1916).

[11] See Shand, *The Foundations of Character*, p. 268f, above cited.

[12] Same, p. 448.

[13] Hocking, *Human Nature and Its Remaking*, above cited, p. 376.

[14] In *Young India* for Nov. 5, 1925, Gandhi wrote in answer to a question why he had enlisted men for service in World War I:

"As a citizen not then and not even now, a reformer leading an agitation against the institution of war, I had to advise and lead men who believed in war but who from cowardice, or from base motives or from anger against the British Government refrained from enlisting. I did not hesitate to advise them that so long as they believed in war and professed loyalty to the British constitution they were in duty bound to support it by enlistment. Though I do not believe in the use of arms, and though it is contrary to the religion of *Ahimsa* which I profess, I should not hesitate to join an agitation for a repeal of the debasing Arms Act which I have considered amongst the blackest crimes of the British Government against India. I do not believe in retaliation, but I did not hesitate to tell the villagers of Bettiah four years ago that they who knew nothing of *Ahimsa* were guilty of cowardice in failing to defend the honour of their women-folk and their property by force of arms. And I have not hesitated, as the correspondent should know, only recently to tell the Hindus that if they do not believe in out-and-out *Ahimsa* and cannot practise it, they will be guilty of a crime against their religion and humanity if they fail to defend by force of arms the honour of their women against any kidnapper who chooses to take away their women." M. K. Gandhi, *Nonviolence in Peace and War*, vol. 1, p. 49f. (Ahmedabad, India: Navajivan 1948).

CHAPTER THREE

[1] W. H. H. Rivers, *Instinct and the Unconscious*, p. 93 (New York: Macmillan 1920). Also Trotter, above cited, p. 82.

[2] Baudouin, above cited.

[3] See Burrow, above cited.

[4] Rivers, above cited, p. 91f.

[5] Edward Alsworth Ross, *Social Psychology*, pp. 120, 126, 130, 136 (New York: Macmillan 1909).

[6] Karl von Clausewitz, *On War*, vol. 1, p. 99 (New York: Dutton 1914).

[7] P. 78. London: Hugh Rees Ltd. 1905.

[8] See W. B. Pillsbury & C. L. Meade, *The Psychology of Language*, p. 6 (New York: Appleton 1928).

[9] See C. K. Ogden & I. A. Richards, *The Meaning of Meaning*, especially chapters on "Sign Situations" and "Symbol Situations" (New York: Harcourt Brace 1927). Also I. A. Richards, *Principles of Literary Criticism*, Chapter 21 (New York: Harcourt Brace 1926).

[10] See H. Vaihinger, *The Philosophy of "As If"* (New York: Harcourt Brace 1924) for a discussion of the "fruitful fiction" and its operation.

[11] See Sante de Sanctis, *Religious Conversion* (New York: Harcourt Brace 1927).

[12] Richards, *Principles of Literary Criticism*, above cited.

[13] Rivers, above cited, p. 54.

[14] See M. P. Follett, *Creative Experience*, p. 62 (New York: Longmans Green 1924).

[15] Same, p. 157ff. See also Bondurant, above cited, p. 196f., pp. 218ff.

[16] Same, p. 171.

CHAPTER FOUR

[1] See Crile, above cited, and Hocking, *Morale and Its Enemies*, above cited.

[2] See W. M. Marston, *Emotions of Normal People*, Chapter 17 (New York: Harcourt Brace 1928).

[3] William Alanson White, *Mechanisms of Character Formation*, p. 274 (New York: Macmillan 1916). See also pp. 73, 278. Also, Erich Fromm, *Man for Himself* (New York: Rinehart 1947).

[4] See William James, *The Principles of Psychology,* vol. 1, p. 125 (New York: Dover Publications 1950).

[5] See C. F. Andrews, *India and the Simon Report* (New York: Macmillan 1930).

[6] Pp. 188-191.

[7] Trotter, above cited, p. 125.

[8] Same, p. 123.

CHAPTER FIVE

[1] Kempf, above cited, p. 79ff. *See* also Shand, above cited, pp. 214-217, p. 250, and Fromm, *Man for Himself,* above cited.

[2] Kempf, above cited.

[3] See Crile, above cited.

[4] I. P. Pavlov, *Lectures on Conditioned Reflexes* (New York: International Publishers 1928). *See* also John B. Watson, *Behaviorism* (New York: Norton 1925).

[5] Marshal Foch, *Principles of War,* p. 99 (New York: H. K. Fly 1918).

[6] See James, above cited, vol. 1, chapter on "Habit."

[7] Quoted in C. F. Andrews, "The Coming Crisis in India," in *The New Republic,* April 3, 1929.

[8] See Ernst Toller, *Man and the Masses* (New York: Doubleday, Page 1924).

[9] Bertrand Russell, *Justice in War Time* (Chicago: Open Court 1924). See also Stephen King-Hall, *Defense in the Nuclear Age* (Nyack, N. Y.: Fellowship 1959).

CHAPTER SIX

[1] Foch, above cited, p. 316.

[2] Sir Ian Hamilton, *The Soul and Body of the Army,* p. 134 (London: Edward Arnold 1921).

[3] Lieut. General August von Caemmerer, *The Development of Strategical Science* (London: Hugh Rees 1905).

[4] Major General Sir F. Maurice, *British Strategy,* p. 67 (London: Constable 1929).

[5] B. H. Liddell Hart, *The Real War,* p. 506 (Boston: Little, Brown 1930). See also Liddell Hart, *Strategy,* pp. 164, 228, 235 (New York: Praeger 1954).

[6] Hocking, *Morale and Its Enemies,* above cited, p. 151.

[7] Same. See also Bartlett, above cited.

[8] Rivers, above cited, p. 219; see also p. 211f. During World War I, Rivers was on the staff of a British hospital treating "shell shock" and other nervous disorders of soldiers.

[9] Clausewitz, above cited, vol. 1, p. 99; Caemmerer, above cited, p. 78.

[10] T. H. Proctor, *The Motives of the Soldier,* 31 International Journal of Ethics, p. 26 (Oct. 1920).

[11] See Hocking, *Morale and Its Enemies,* above cited, p. 99.

[12] Lieut. Col. L. C. Andrews, *Military Manpower* (New York: Dutton 1920).

[13] Bartlett, above cited, pp. 172-175; Hocking, above cited, p. 159.

[14] See B. H. Liddell Hart, *Strategy,* above cited, p. 370.

[15] B. H. Liddell Hart, "Armament and Its Future Uses," p. 652 in *Yale Review,* July 1930.

[16] J. F. C. Fuller, *The Reformation of War,* pp. 64, 70 (New York: Dutton 1923).

[17] See Salvador de Madariaga, *Englishmen, Frenchmen, Spaniards: an Essay in Comparative Psychology,* pp. 27, 58 (New York: Oxford 1928).

[18] Salvador de Madariaga, *Disarmament,* p. 60 (New York: Coward-Mc-Cann 1929).

[19] Fuller, above cited, p. 46.

[20] See Andrews, above cited.

[21] Clausewitz, above cited, vol. 3, p. 209.

[22] *The Autobiography of Kwame Nkrumah,* pp. 53, 75, 103, 110-112, 196-198 (New York: Nelson 1957).

[23] See Allan A. Hunter, *Courage in Both Hands,* pp. 37-40, above cited, and William James, *The Varieties of Religious Experience,* p. 359 (New York: Modern Library 1936). For other books, see the *Bibliography* cited in the notes to Chapter One, above.

CHAPTER SEVEN

[1] In William James, *Memories and Studies* (New York: Longmans, Green 1911). An abridgement of the essay is more conveniently available in Henry Steele Commager, *Living Ideas in America* (New York: Harper 1951).

[2] Walter Lippmann, "The Political Equivalent of War," in the *Atlantic Monthly,* August 1928, p. 181f.

[3] A. A. Walser, "Air Power," in *The Nineteenth Century and After* (London), April 1923, p. 598.

[4] Clausewitz, above cited, vol. 3, p. 210. See also B. H. Liddell Hart, *The Real War,* p. 446 (Boston: Little, Brown 1930).

[5] Napoleon, *Maxims of War,* Maxim XVI (Kansas City, Mo.: Hudson-Kimberly 1902).

[6] Quoted in Hamilton, above cited, p. 134.

[7] Foch, above cited, p. 316.

[8] King-Hall, above cited, p. 110.

[9] See articles and editorials and book reviews in *Saturday Review* (New York) during 1955-58, also talk by P. M. S. Blackett, titled "Alamo Heretic," reprinted in *The Listener* (London) for Sept. 11, 1958.

[10] See Edward Glover, *War, Sadism and Pacifism* (London: Allen and Unwin 1933). For another view of sadism and masochism, see Fromm, *Man for Himself,* above cited.

[11] Foch, above cited, p. 32.

CHAPTER EIGHT

[1] See Randolph Bourne, "The State," in *Untimely Papers* (New York: Huebsch 1919); L. P. Jacks, "The Insane Root: War and the State," *Atlantic Monthly,* January 1917; Lewis Mumford, "Wardom and the State," *The Dial,* October 4, 1919; Johan Huizinga, "Regina Regnis Lupi," in *In the Shadow of Tomorrow* (New York: Norton 1936); [The foregoing also appear in Waldo R. Browne, ed., *Leviathan in Crisis* (New York: Viking 1946).] Also, Bertrand Russell, *Why Men Fight* (New York: Century 1916); Reinhold Niebuhr, *Moral Man and Immoral Society* (New York: Scribners 1932); Sigmund Freud, *Reflections on War and Death* (New York: Moffat Yard 1918); and various writings of John Dewey, Admiral A. T. Mahan, Leo Tolstoi and Thorstein Veblen.

[2] Clausewitz, above cited, vol. 1, p. xxviii and vol. 3, p. 121. See also Madariaga, *Disarmament,* above cited, p. 59f.

[3] The great Indian philosopher, Aurobindo Gose, writes:

"So long as war does not become psychologically impossible, it will remain, or, if banished, for a while, return. War itself, it is hoped, will end war; the expense, the horror, the butchery, the disturbance of tranquil life, the whole confused sanguinary madness of the thing has reached or will reach such colossal proportions that the human race will fling the monstrosity behind it in weariness and disgust. But weariness and disgust, horror and pity, even the opening of the eyes to reason by the practical facts of the waste of human life and energy and the harm and extravagance are not permanent factors; they last only while the lesson is fresh. Afterwards, there is forgetfulness; human nature recuperates and recovers the instincts that were temporarily dominated. . . . War is no longer, perhaps, a biological necessity, but is still a psychological necessity; what is within must manifest itself outside.

". . . Only when man has developed not merely a fellow-feeling with all men, but a dominant sense of unity and commonalty, only when he is aware of them not merely as brothers—that is a fragile bond—but in a large universal consciousness, can the phenomenon of war, with whatever weapons, pass out of his life without the possibility of return."—Aurobindo Gose, *War and Self-Determination* (Calcutta: S. Ghose 1922).

This opinion is in substance echoed by Bertrand Russell:

"The supposed economic causes of war, except in the case of certain capitalistic enterprises, are in the nature of a rationalization; people wish to fight, and they therefore persuade themselves that it is to their interest to do so. The important question, then, is the psychological one—"Why do people wish to fight?" And this leads on from war to a host of other questions concerning impulses to cruelty and oppression in general. These questions in their turn involve a study of the origins of the malevolent passions, and thence of psychoanalysis and the theory of education. . . .

"The basis of international anarchy is man's proneness to fear and hatred. This is also the basis of economic disputes; for the love of power, which is at their root, is generally an embodiment of fear."—Bertrand Russell, "What I Believe," in *The Forum* (New York), Sept. 1929.

[4] Reinhold Niebuhr, "A Critique of Pacifism," in *The Atlantic Monthly,* May 1927, reprinted in Reinhold Niebuhr, *Love and Justice* (D. B. Robertson, ed.) (Philadelphia: Westminster Press 1957).

[5] Leon Trotsky, "Democracy, Pacifism and Imperialism," in N. Lenin and L. Trotsky, *The Proleterian Revolution in Russia* (L. Fraina, ed.), p. 196f. (New York: The Communist Press 1918).

[6] Madariaga, *Disarmament,* above cited, pp. 42, 45, 48, 56, 61, 198. But this need not mean a super-State with supremely powerful armed forces. As soon as one nation organizes itself for nonviolent resistance and wins an international struggle by those tactics, there will be imitators, and our present international relationships will change completely.

[7] See my books *Which Way Lies Hope?* and *A Philosophy of Indian Economic Development* (Ahmedabad, India: Navajivan 1958).

[8] See C. Y. Shepard, "Diversification of Crops," in *Tropical Agriculture,* vol. 2, no. 5 (St. Augustine, Trinidad, B. W. I.: Imperial College of Tropical Agriculture).

[9] See Frank Geary, *Land Tenure and Unemployment* (London: Allen & Unwin 1925).

[10] See Curtis Bok, *Star Wormwood* (New York: Knopf 1959); Alfred Hassler, *Diary of a Self-Made Convict* (Nyack, N. Y.: Fellowship 1958); Giles Playfair & Derrick Sington, *The Offenders* (New York: Simon & Shuster 1957); Arthur Koestler, *Reflections on Hanging* (New York: Macmillan 1958); George Godwin, *Crime and Social Action* (London: Watts 1956); Ralph S. Baney, *We Call Them Criminals* (New York: Appleton-Century-Crofts 1958); Erle Stanley Gardner, *The Court of Last Resort* (New York: Sloane 1953); G. M. Sykes, *The Society of Captives* (Princeton: Princeton Univ. Press 1959).

[11] See Bernard Shaw, *Imprisonment* (New York: Dodd, Mead 1925).

[12] See Henry A. Cotton, *The Defective, Delinquent and Insane,* in Dr. Cotton's 1953 report as Medical Director and Director of Research of the New Jersey State Hospital. See also Joseph Needham, "Biochemistry and Mental Phenomena," an Appendix in *The Creator Spirit* by C. E. Raven, pp. 296-299. (London: Martin Hopkinson 1927).

[13] Perhaps even psychiatry itself needs reform for this purpose. See Burrow, *The Social Basis of Consciousness,* above cited.

[14] See Hunter, above cited. Also Danilo Dolci, *Palermo* (London: MacGibbon & Kee 1958). There is a fine example in the work of Danilo Dolci the "Italian Gandhi," among impoverished bandits. See Giovanni Pioli, "Crusade Against Poverty," in *Fellowship,* March 1957.

[15] See Hunter, above cited; also Allan A. Hunter, *Three Trumpets Sound* (New York: Association Press 1939).

[16] See M. K. Gandhi, *Young India, 1919-1922,* pp. 1116, 1117, 1118, 1120-22, 1125 (New York: B. W. Huebsch 1923). Also Gandhi, "Some Rules of Satyagraha" in *Young India* (newspaper), Feb. 27, 1930.

CHAPTER NINE

[1] See *Encyclopaedia Brittanica,* 14th ed., esp. articles on "Hormones" and "Smell" and "Taste."

[2] See Max Verworn, *Irritability,* pp. 209-234. (New Haven, Conn.: Yale University Press 1913).

[3] See L. J. Boyd, *A Study of the Simile Principle in Medicine,* pp. 326-361 (Philadelphia: Boericke & Tafel 1936).

[4] Same, pp. 335-361.

[5] Same.

[6] See Sheldon & Eleanor Glueck, *500 Criminal Careers* (New York: Knopf 1930); Robert H. Gault, *Criminology* (New York: Heath 1932); Amos O. Squire, *Sing Sing Doctor* (New York: Doubleday, Doran 1935); Margaret Wilson, *The Crime of Punishment* (New York: Barnes & Noble 1946); Mary Gordon, *Penal Discipline* (London: Routledge 1922); John Lewis Gillin, *Taming the Criminal* (New York: Macmillan 1931). See also footnote 10, Chapter 8 above.

[7] See W. C. Allee, *The Social Life of Animals* (New York: Norton 1938).

[8] See Pyarelal, *Mahatma Gandhi: The Last Phase* (Ahmadabad, India: Navajivan 1958).

[9] Same; also B. R. Nanda, *The Life of Gandhi* (Boston: Beacon 1959).

[10] See Alfred North Whitehead, *Adventures of Ideas,* pp. 31, 53, 105, 108, 205 (New York: Macmillan 1933).

[11] See Gerald Heard, *The Source of Civilization* (New York: Harper 1937).

[12] From "Over the Carnage Rose Prophetic a Voice," in *Leaves of Grass* (New York: Modern Library 1940).

[13] See Wolfgang Köhler, *Gestalt Psychology,* New York: Liveright 1947; W. D. Ellis, ed., *A Source Book of Gestalt Psychology* (New York: Harcourt Brace 1938).

[14] The processes of persuasion are both subtle and complex. We can realize better how complex they are if we make a list of some of the factors which undoubtedly take part in initiating, influencing or determining actions. Bodily condition, for example, is one of these. If one is sick, he will not undertake certain actions, or if he does he will usually do them poorly, or be unable to persist long, or maybe his judgment will be poor. One's emotions initiate or influence certain types of action. If he is hungry he acts one way; if fearful, another; if happy, still another. Some influential factors are:

assumptions
perceptions
knowledge
sentiments
prejudices
beliefs
hopes
affections and loyalties
conflicts of loyalties
desires
conflicts of desires
intellectual energy
ability to coordinate
    ideas with action
past experience
sense of probability
judgment
imagination
speed, range, clearness and
    depth of intelligence

trust
love of truth
persistence
habits
foresight
planning ability
economic motives
flexibility in interpretations or in
    fresh integrations of meaning
formal training
desire for consistency
desire for order
clearness of ideas of order
speed and ease of learning
one's picture of oneself and de-
    sire to play the part
egoism
accuracy, detail, range and du-
    ration of memory

In order to persuade an opponent, one must use powers that will alter a controlling portion of the foregoing factors in him in such a way as to result in a more fully realized unity of purpose and energy than before.

Space in this edition is too limited to permit detailed analysis of the comparative effects of violence and nonviolence on each of the above-listed factors entering into persuasion. But as one brief instance, careful psychological studies have shown that even bare perceptions have in them an element of interpretation. Walking along a road in the twilight, a calm person will see in the roadway a bit of old rope, while a nervous person will see in the same place a snake. Kindness and nonviolence help to create states of mind and feeling which promote true interpretations and perceptions. In various places, we have suggested how such analyses may be made, and must leave the actual making of them to the reader's imagination. But it is safe to say that, in relation to the welfare of society and cooperative action among its members, a sense of unity, gentle kindness, and nonviolent resistance to evil affect every one of the above-named factors favorably. On the other hand, violence and coercion affect every one of them unfavorably. Nonviolence promotes cooperation for social benefit; coercion decreases such cooperation. Nonviolence and love are persuasive.

15 See E. F. M. Durbin & J. Bowlby, *Personal Aggressiveness and War* (New York: Columbia University Press 1940).

16 See Dollard, Doob, *et al., Frustration and Aggression* (New Haven: Yale 1961); also Durbin & Bowlby, above cited.

17 See D. W. Harding, *The Impulse to Dominate* (London: Allen & Unwin 1941).

18 Same.

19 See I. Barnard, *The Functions of the Executive* (Cambridge, Mass.: Harvard 1940).

20 See Richard M. Brickner, M.D., *Is Germany Curable?* (Philadelphia: Lippincott 1943).

CHAPTER TEN

1 The foregoing two paragraphs are taken from Chapter IX of my book *The Self Beyond Yourself* (Philadelphia: Lippincott 1956).

2 See Pearl Buck, *Of Men and Women* (New York: John Day 1941).

CHAPTER ELEVEN

1 Military training has hitherto laid great emphasis on developing habits of absolute obedience, but now with the growth of mechanized armies unthinking obedience is less important. An airplane pilot fighting in the sky, or two men alone in a tank advancing in battle a thousand yards away from any other unit of their army, need general understanding and initiative more than blind obedience. So also of a soldier, shooting rocket missiles. Instead of the old-fashioned soldier's strong habit of blind obedience, the nonviolent resister needs a strong and clear sense of the values held in common with his fellow believers. See Edward T. Dixon, *The Guidance of Conduct* (London: Kegan Paul 1928).

[2] See A. R. Luria, *The Nature of Human Conflicts* (New York: Liveright 1932), especially Chapter XII on "The Control of Behavior"; H. G. Wyatt, *The Psychology of Intelligence and Will* (New York: Harcourt Brace 1930); Francis Aveling, *Personality and Will* (London: Nisbet 1931).

[3] See Harold Burrows, *The Cultivation of Sentiment*, London: Leonard Parsons 1929; Shand, *The Foundations of Character,* above cited; Sir Martin Conway, *The Crowd in Peace and War* (New York: Longmans, Green 1915).

[4] See Heard, *The Source of Civilization,* above cited; Aldous Huxley, *Ends and Means* (New York: Harper 1937); Kenneth Boulding, *The Image* (Ann Arbor: University of Michigan 1956); Fromm, *The Art of Loving,* above cited; Durbin and Bowlby, above cited; Mark A. May, *A Social Psychology of War and Peace* (New Haven: Yale 1943; Ian D. Suttie, *The Origins of Love and Hate* (London: Kegan Paul 1949); Lewis Mumford, *The Transformations of Man* (New York: Harper 1957); Gandhi, *Nonviolence in Peace and War,* above cited; King-Hall, above cited; Bradford Lyttle, *Essays on Nonviolent Action* (5729 Dorchester Ave., Chicago 37, Ill.: Bradford Lyttle 1959).

Religious aspects of pacifism are treated in G. H. C. Macgregor, *The New Testament Basis of Pacifism* (Nyack, N. Y.: Fellowship 1959); Culbert G. Rutenber, *The Dagger and the Cross* (Nyack, N. Y.: Fellowship 1958); Leo Tolstoi, *The Law of Love and the Law of Violence* (New York: R. Field 1948).

For further reading see the *Bibliography on War, Pacifism, Nonviolence and Related Studies* (Nyack, N. Y.: Fellowship 1959). Pamphlets on these subjects are obtainable from the Fellowship of Reconciliation, Nyack, N. Y.; The War Resisters League, 5 Beekman St., New York 38; Women's International League for Peace and Freedom, 2006 Walnut St., Philadelphia 3, Pa.; some publications of the UN and UNESCO and organizations in England.

[5] Regarding the psychological value of large meetings, processions and demonstrations, see Conway, *The Crowd in Peace and War,* above cited.

[6] For discussion of the value of smallness of organizations see Graham Wallas, *The Great Society,* pp. 297, 300, 309, 314, 332, 337, 348, 350, 360 (New York: Macmillan 1914); also his *Human Nature in Politics,* pp. 44-52 and 270-274 (New York: Knopf 1921); also Heard, *The Social Substance of Religion* (New York: Harcourt Brace 1931); also R. H. Tawney, *The Acquisitive Society* (New York: Harcourt Brace 1946).

[7] See Noelle Davies, *Education for Life* (London: Williams & Norgate 1931).

[8] See Thomas W. Surette, *Music and Life* (Boston: Houghton Mifflin 1917); Max Schoen, *The Effects of Music* (New York: Harcourt, Brace 1929); Charles M. Diserens, *The Influence of Music on Behavior* (Princeton: Princeton University Press 1926; William van de Wall, *Music in Institutions* (New York: Russell Sage Foundation 1936); James L. Mursell, *Human Values in Music Education* (New York and Chicago: Silver, Burdette 1934); A. Headmistress, "Experiment in Educating the Mind Through the Body," in the *Hibbert Journal,* Jan. 1933, vol. 31, pp. 271-223; H. Henly, "Prison Music," in the *Atlantic Monthly,* July 1929, vol. 144, pp. 69-76; A. Fellows, "Creative Music and the Bad Boy," in *Progressive Education,* April, 1931, vol. 8, pp. 348-349; Suzanne K. Langer, *Feeling and Form* (New York: Scribner 1953).

[9] Lists of folk songs will be found in the article on "Song" in George Grove, *Dictionary of Music and Musicians* (New York: St. Martin's 1959) and in the *Oxford History of Music* (new introductory volume). Good collections of English and American folk songs are published by Oliver Ditson Co., Boston, Mass.; G. Schirmer, New York; Theodore Presser, Philadelphia; Lyon & Healy, Chicago; Oxford University Press, London & New York; Boosey, Hawkes & Belwin, New York; Carl Fischer, New York & Boston; and others.

[10] They would be wise to choose hymns by such old composers as Palestrina, Vittoria, Bach, Gibbons, Byrd, Purcell, John Goss or Samuel Wesley. See also the collection, *Hymns of Hope and Courage* (Boston, Mass.: Congregational Publishing House).

[11] See Bliss Carmen, *The Making of Personality* (Boston: L. C. Page 1908); T. & M. W. Kinney, *The Dance* (New York: Stokes 1914); W. D. Humbley, *Tribal Dancing and Social Development* (London: Witherby 1922); Havelock Ellis, *The Dance of Life* (New York: Grosset & Dunlap 1956), especially Chapter II; Henry J. Watt, *The Sensory Basis and Structure of Knowledge* (London: Methuen 1925); Emile Jaques-Dalcroze, *Rhythm, Music and Education* (New York: Putnam 1921); Jo Pennington, *The Importance of Dancing Rhythm* (New York: Putnam 1925); Luria, *The Nature of Human Conflicts,* pp. 211, 44, above cited.

[12] Collections of folk dance music and instructions are published by A. S. Barnes & Co., 11 East 36th St., New York; G. Schirmer & Co., 3 East 43rd St., New York; Summy-Birchard Pub. Co., 1834 Ridge Ave., Evanston, Ill.; Curwen, Inc., 1701 Chestnut St., Philadelphia, Pa.; Novello, Ltd., London, England; Longmans, Green, 55 Fifth Ave., New York; Evans Bros., Ltd., London; Cambridge University Press.

[13] Some books and passages tending to promote a sense of wide human unity and tolerance are: Ruth Benedict, *Patterns of Culture* (New York: Penguin Books 1946); Jules Payot, *The Education of the Will,* 13th American ed. (New York: Funk & Wagnalls 1920); Rabindrinath Tagore, *Sadhana* (New York: Macmillan 1913); Leo Tolstoi, *Twenty-Three Tales* (New York: Oxford University Press 1945); Robert Browning, *The Ring and the Book* (New York: Norton 1958); Holy Bible, New Testament, 1 Corinthians 13; Earl of Lytton, *New Treasure* (London: Allen & Unwin 1934); Jan C. Smuts, *Holism and Evolution* (New York: Macmillan 1926); Edward Carpenter, *Towards Democracy* (London: Allen & Unwin 1931); Whitman, *Leaves of Grass,* above cited; A. N. Whitehead, *Science and the Modern World* (New York: Macmillan 1926); Heard, *The Source of Civilization,* above cited; J. B. Bury, *A History of Freedom of Thought* (New York: Oxford 1952); Hendrik Willem Van Loon, *The Story of Tolerance* (New York: Liveright 1940); William Penn, "The Great Case for Liberty of Conscience," in *Select Works,* vol. 3 (London: W. Phillips 1825); John Stuart Mill, *On Liberty* (Chicago: Regnery); Basil Mathews, *The Jew and the World Ferment* (New York: Friendship ·Press 1935); James Weldon Johnson, *Along this Way* (New York: Viking Press 1933).

[14] For example, the lives and sayings of Buddha, MoTi, Akhnaton, Lao Tzü, Jesus, St. Francis of Assissi, Menno Simons, George Fox, William Penn, John Woolman, William Lloyd Garrison, Henry David Thoreau, Percy Bysshe Shelley, Leo Tolstoi, Eugene V. Debs, Jane Addams, Olive Schreimer, Emily Hobhouse, Albert Schweitzer, Romain Rolland, Mahatma Gandhi, Toyohiko

Kagawa. See also these accounts of the British and American conscientious objectors during two world wars: J. W. Graham, *Conscription and Conscience* (London: Allen & Unwin 1922); Julian Bell, ed., *We Did Not Fight* (London: Cobden-Sanderson 1935); Norman Thomas, *Is Conscience a Crime?* (New York: Vanguard 1928); Harold S. Gray, *Character Bad* (New York: Harper 1934); Ernest L. Meyer, *Hey, Yellowbacks!* (New York: John Day 1930); James Peck, *We Who Would Not Fight* (New York: Lyle Stuart 1958).

[15] For some instances see Clarence Marsh Case, *Nonviolent Coercion* (New York: Century 1923); Carl Heath, *Pacifism in Time of War* (London: Headley 1915); Hunter, *Courage in Both Hands*, above cited; Jawaharlal Nehru, *Nehru on Gandhi* (New York: John Day 1949); John Haynes Holmes, *New Wars for Old* (New York: Dodd, Mead 1916); Fry, above cited; Bart de Ligt, *The Conquest of Violence* (New York: Dutton 1938); Erica and Roderic Dunkerly, *The Arm of God* (Edinborough: Oliphants 1917).

[16] See the historical books listed in note 4, above; also A. N. Whitehead, *Adventures of Ideas* (New York: Macmillan 1933); Heard, *The Source of Civilization*, above cited.

[17] For the psychological necessity of this, see Luria, *The Nature of Human Conflicts;* Hocking, *Morale and Its Enemies;* Bartlett, *Psychology and the Soldier,* all above cited.

[18] See A. N. Whitehead, *Leadership in a Free Society* (Cambridge: Harvard 1936).

[19] See G. Elliott Smith, *Essays on the Evolution of Man* (London: Benn 1931); Frederic W. Jones and Stanley D. Porteus, *The Matrix of the Mind* (Honolulu, Hawaii: University Press Assoc. 1928).

[20] See Nathanial Shaler, *The Neighbor* (Boston: Houghton, Mifflin 1904); Shaler, *The Individual,* Chapter VI, D (New York: Appleton 1900).

[21] See the educational system of Sanderson of Oundle School, England described in Frederick Peterson, *Creative Re-education* (New York: Putnam 1936).

[22] Maurice, p. 4, above cited; J. L. Garvin, article on "Capitalism," Encyclopaedia Britannica, 14th ed.; John Dewey, *Human Nature and Conduct,* p. 115 (New York: Holt 1922); "The Position and Tasks of the Socialist International" in Lenin, *Works,* Vol. XVIII, p. 88 (New York: International 1942). The distinguished anthropologist, Bronislaw Malinowski, agreed by implication, since he said that the abolition of war would require great changes in individuals, in the organization of the state, and in our cultural outlook. See his article, "The Deadly Issues," in the *Atlantic Monthly,* Dec. 1936.

[23] See A. D. Richie, *The Natural History of Thought,* p. 69 (London: Longmans, Green 1936).

[24] See Roy Hilton, *Sold Out to the Future* (New York: Harper 1935).

[25] See Köhler and Ellis, both above cited. Also Kurt Koffka, *Principles of Gestalt Psychology* (New York: Harcourt Brace 1915) and Raymond H. Wheeler, *The Science of Psychology,* pp. 151, 243 (New York: Crowell 1929).

[26] In the "Timaeus," § 48A, *Timaeus and Critias* (New York: Pantheon 1945).

INDEX